Pra

MW00747921

Winning Them
With Prayer

*This book is powerful and exactly what I needed!
Thanks for the prompting of the Holy Spirit and your obedience to
Him! May the Lord continue to do a work in you and through you
in Jesus' name. Amen.* — Jessica B.

Amen and AMEN! This is a huge encouragement. — Mandy G.

Powerful revelation to me. — Ramona F.

*AMEN AMEN AMEN AMEN AMEN!!!! Said it five times because
there are five of us in my family!!! Lynn, I LOVE this message!*
— Jenni R.

*Thank you for sharing your knowledge of the spiritual realm
with us, Lynn!* — Brittany

AMEN! Thank you, Lynn; I will begin using this prayer today!
— Karla O.

*As I read one of your prayers aloud, I could sense the power of God. It
is my declaration. Amen. I thank God this was released so that many
could hear what saith the Lord.* — Jaimie H.

*I am so thankful for words of encouragement, as without them I feel
I might grow too weary of the battle.* — Sharon

*Absolutely beautiful. I how love you show two different examples in
the chapter about expectations. We must believe AND follow up with
actions and faith. Thanks for the reminder!* — Tiffany C.

winning
them with
PRAYER

Lynn Donovan
Dineen Miller
SUM Community

Three Keys Publishing

Winning Them With Prayer

Published by Three Keys Publishing
Temecula, California, U.S.A.
www.threekeysministries.org
Printed in the U.S.A.

Cover Design: Lynn Donovan & Dineen Miller
Interior Design: Dineen Miller
Editor: Eileen Key

This collection is dedicated to
Abba Father, Jesus Christ and the Holy Spirit.

It is also dedicated to the men and women who walk in faith
while they pray for the salvation of their loved ones.

Contents

Introduction

The prayer of a righteous person is powerful and effective.
— James 5:16

The journey of the spiritually mismatched is a joyous adventure. It is also a challenging path to navigate. In the early years of our married life, we learn to grow in our faith. Then as we begin to mature in faith, we find ourselves struggling within our marriage as our love for Christ flourishes and our spouse remains aloof to the notion of a loving God. Although we may have walked this road for decades or for only a handful of months, we are committed to honoring our marriage and honoring our Lord Jesus.

We are the unequally yoked.

We believe in the teaching of Paul who wrote in *2 Corinthians 6:14 — Do not be yoked together with unbelievers.* However, many of us find ourselves living spiritually mismatched because we came to faith after our marriage or through several other circumstances and choices. Our hope rests on 1 Peter 3:1 that our spouses may be won over to faith in Jesus Christ.

In our unique marriages, we face a host of struggles such as loneliness, parenting differences, church attendance, tithing, moral conflicts and faith practices to name a few. However, we remain steadfast, following Jesus and empowered by His fathomless love and faithfulness. Our faith moves us forward. We learn to love others well, we forgive freely, we rise above the struggles and discover we can *thrive* in our marriage and family as well as in our faith.

We learn to thrive because we learn to PRAY!

This book encapsulates our hope for our faith and marriage, exercised through prayer. We begin with thirteen authoritative prayer strategies that the Holy Spirit is revealing to the church in this season. The prayer strategies include scriptures, prayers and living examples of how to pray in faith with power and authority to defeat the demonic realm, to release the Kingdom of God and to contend for the salvation of our loved ones. There is also a place to write down your specific and personal prayers and to develop the strategies, thus empowering your prayer life.

Additionally, this book is a collection of prayers written by real people who are living and loving Jesus and their unbelieving spouse. (Actually, we prefer to call our spouses 'pre-believers'!) The stories and prayers are authentic. They are relevant to impart wisdom and encouragement to those who travel the spiritually mismatched journey.

Our years of praying have availed much in our lives. We bear witness to the truth of James 5:16. We have observed the miraculous in answer to our humble prayers, spoken in moments of quiet intimacy with the King. Yet we live with the tension that our prayer for our spouse's salvation remains unanswered. Often it's the answers to our many other prayers which fuels our hearts and faith to remain faithful, trusting for our spouse and unsaved family members to come to faith in Jesus.

We have also been transformed by prayer. Did you know that according to Dr. Caroline Leaf, a Cognitive Neuroscientist, that scientists have actually proven that we are more intelligent and higher functioning when we pray and worship? She wrote in her blog how prayer affects the brain. It has been found that 12 minutes of daily focused prayer over an eight-week period can change the brain to such an extent that it can be measured on a brain scan. This type of prayer increases activity in the brain areas associated with social interaction, compassion and sensitivity to others. It also increases frontal lobe activity, focus and intentionally (June 1, 2015). Our prayers change our heart, our soul, our physical body and influence our environments, which can lead to life-change in ourselves and our prayers impact others.

We believe in the power of prayer!

The prayers in this book are diverse and cover various aspects of faith, the spiritual realm, and Scripture, and they focus on our relationship with God as well as our marriage and family. In the pages, you will encounter prayers of warfare, as the unequally yoked are intentional prayer warriors. There are prayers of intercession as well as prayers for provision. These prayers will soothe your heart, heal wounds and build up your faith. The prayers in this book are humble, trustworthy words spoken to our good Heavenly Father and His Son, Jesus, through the

Holy Spirit. They are offerings and petitions to the King, and we are convinced they are heard and moved upon from heaven.

If you have picked up this book looking for prayer strategies, you will not be disappointed. Read through the stories and speak the prayers aloud, reading them often. Place your name or the names of your spouse, children, or others into the prayers. Personalize the prayers and speak them out with heartfelt conviction and faith.

And as you turn the pages, please know that as you read, you are covered with prayer. You are loved, you are seen and you are heard by our kind and compassionate Savior, Jesus Christ. Collectively, we cover you with prayers of intercession and faith for the full salvation of your home in like fashion to the home of Cornelius the Centurion.

He will bring you a message through which you and all your household will be saved. — Acts 11:14

We love you.

Lynn Donovan & Dineen Miller and the SUM Community

Meet Lynn & Dineen
Meet The SUM Community

Let us hold unswervingly to the hope we profess, for he who promised is faithful. And let us consider how we may spur one another on toward love and good deeds, not giving up meeting together, as some are in the habit of doing, but encouraging one another—and all the more as you see the Day approaching.
—Hebrews 10: 23-25

Hello! We are Lynn Donovan and Dineen Miller. We are ordinary women who believe in Jesus and are married to pre-believers. We have been walking the road of the spiritually mismatched, each for more than 25 years. We have travailed through the challenges of faith and marriage, choosing to love our husbands and Jesus, equipped with Holy Spirit power and with authentic joy. We are imperfect women who rise every morning adorned in hope. And we are women of prayer. And one more thing—both of our husband's names are Mike. Could that be a coincidence?

In 2006, Lynn launched the blog, SpirituallyUnequalMarriage. com, in an effort to encourage and connect with others who are also unequally yoked in marriage. Shortly thereafter, Dineen came on board and the two of us have been writing together ever since. We have connected with thousands of God's Children who live all around the world. Our hearts are moved by the Lord to pray for one another and for the believers we meet online.

In 2011, at the request of the SUM community (acronym of our blog name), we released our first Bible study, *Winning Him Without Words: 10 Keys to Thriving in Your Spiritually Mismatched Marriage*. A few years later, a second Bible study, *Not Alone: Trusting God to Help You Raise Godly Kids In A Spiritual Mismatched Marriage*, was released. The core of our ministry is to equip the Saints to thrive in the love of our Father and to love others well.

The thousands of believers who visit the website are the SUMites, who also study the books, participate in our speaking events and online teaching. They are amazing men and women of God who live out the truths of Scripture in their marriages every day of the week. They are ordinary people of faith who serve an extraordinary God. They love their spouse and kids, and they also aspire to live by the unerring principals of the Word of God.

They are the heroes of this book!

They are the heroes of heaven!

Many of their genuine and compelling prayers are included in this collection. They share their faith, families and heart in these pages, with hope that you will be encouraged and filled with expectation for your marriage.

Following each of the prayers, you can read a short bio about the author. Heaven applauds each one, because they volunteered their time, words, prayers and love to add to this compilation. Those of us, who share our lives in these pages, invite you to receive everything we have received from Jesus. So collectively, we, the authors of this prayer book, would like to pray a prayer of blessing over you. Receive it in full faith in Jesus Christ.

We love you,

Lynn, Dineen and the SUM Community

Jesus, today we ask that You would come along side this beloved of Yours who is holding this book. Today, Jesus, we ask that You would bless them with peace (Romans 14:17). Bless them with all that they need to persevere in prayer for the salvation of their loved ones (2 Peter 3:9). Lord, multiply their time, that they can read through this offering completely and let the truths in the pages unfold in their lives (Matthew 14:13-21). Fashion the prayers powerfully, as they read and then inspire them to speak the words aloud in full faith from their hearts over their families. Release warrior angels to harken (Psalm 103:20) unto the Word of God as it is prayed and release the angelic to move in this world for Your purposes and according to Your will. Bless them with the Spirit of Wisdom and Revelation to know Your will better for their lives and faith walk (Ephesians 1:17). Place upon them the gifts of the Holy Spirit so they will be workers in this Great Harvest of the

Age (Luke 10:2).

Lord Jesus, we ask Your protection over this beloved. Lead Your Child to learn and then effectively use the prayer strategies of Heaven. Protect them from all assignments of the enemy. We declare that no weapon formed against them will prosper (Isaiah 54:17). And we declare and stand with them in faith for the salvation of their home (Acts 16:34). We also stand with them for fantastic victories in their lives and ministries. We ask that they will walk in love, joy, peace, patience and all the fruit of the Holy Spirit to Your honor and glory (Galatians 5:22-23).

In Jesus' Mighty Name. AMEN!

Hallelujah!

Visit us at SpirituallyUnequalMarriage.com and join the Harvest Revolution of the SUMites!

Chapter One:
What Is God Speaking To His Church Today?

By Lynn Donovan

Therefore confess your sins to each other and pray for each other so that you may be healed. The prayer of a righteous person is powerful and effective. — James 5:16

The Holy Spirit is speaking the Word – PRAYER!

"Oh man, did she just write – PRAYER?" I wonder, did you just whisper this under your breath?

Let me explain what I believe the Lord is impressing upon His church in this current season.

Prayer.

For years, I served on staff in women's ministry at my local church. I led Bible study groups, I selected studies for our ministry and directed many of the Bible study efforts. In the years serving the church in this capacity, I always found it fascinating as well as disappointing, that if a bible study was offered about prayer, no one signed up. Yep.

Bummer! But true.

However, in this new season of the Lord, I'm discovering that the church attitude is changing. Believers have a growing hunger to understand prayer strategies and to experience powerful prayer and watch God move in response. Today, when I teach on the subject of prayer, the class is well attended. When I post a prayer on Facebook, the prayer is shared. I'm psyched about this transformation in the heart of the Church. Hallelujah!

My friend, now is the time to gain wisdom, knowledge and anointing to pray with power for REAL results! It's the Lord's heart that His children step out of powerless Christianity and walk in their full identity and pray out of our identity.

Sound good?

Good! Let's do it!

Before we continue, let us always remain mindful that prayer is NOT a way to arm twist the Lord. Prayer is a conversation between a Father and His child. It's learning to listen to God and then obeying *His* will.

I want to look at several keys to vibrant prayer as well as "blocks" that keep us from breakthroughs. Because prayer is a unique conversation with the Lord, we likely won't cover every facet of effective prayer. But we will touch on several characteristics that are less well known. Such as:

Praying the Word of God
Belief
Confidence
Our Will
Courage

And finally, we will discuss the "why" when our prayers remain unanswered. And I might throw a few extras in somewhere along the way. Prior to jumping into these specific prayer strategies, it's crucial to understand how we go about creating a prayer life.

Creating a Prayer Way of Life

Everything the Lord has poured into my life over the years is a direct result of my intentional efforts to create time and space to foster intimacy with God. I know that "making time" is often *the* most challenging part of prayer, but even devoting a few minutes a day to prayer can change your life. After years of struggle in my spiritually mismatched marriage, I decided to commit to a daily appointment with the King. At that time, I was raising small children and I also worked full time, so was necessary that I rise early in order that I could have time to pray. I realized God's goodness was evidenced in my life and this fueled my desire to please Him and enabled me to keep my appointment with Him in the morning.

I started reading a Daily Bible. The Word of God changed my life. On June 13, 1998, my mother gave me a 365 Day Daily Bible. This Bible is organized into a daily reading over 365 days a year. It includes reading in the Old Testament, New Testament, a Psalm, and Proverb. The translation is easy reading, *New Living Translation.* I remember the date exactly because the day I began to read, I wrote the date — June 13, 1999 in the margin of my Bible. I have read through the Word every year since.

All these years later, I truly *know* God's Word, because I have read it for myself. His Word abides in me.

A Daily Bible may not be the right fit for your life. You may already have a daily reading practice. Wonderful! However, if you aren't reading daily and want your life to be different in a year from now, start with a daily reading plan. Order a Daily Bible online or head to the bookstore.

Let me add a few thoughts. Daily reading of God's Word may at first feel like dreaded duty. It is a duty to set the alarm 30 minutes earlier to meet with God. It may feel like an obligation to push through the chapters when you are tired. You may consider skipping your time alone with God because you have a million things on your to-do list. However, I will make you a PROMISE.

DUTY WILL TURN TO DESIRE!

When you regularly meet with the Lord through Bible reading and prayer, you will discover that your faith grows exponentially and your life changes so much for the better.

Don't become obsessed with the reading plan itself. Read what you can in 15-20 minutes and then pray. Perhaps you will only read a chapter from the New Testament or a Psalm. Read something every day. When you read a passage, take notice when a line or a word jumps out at you, making an impression and then underline it. Bring the passage to God in prayer for more understanding or revelation.

After my reading, I pick up my prayer journal and begin to pray. Writing sentences in longhand leads my mind to focus on the page and the words that I'm praying to the Lord. Writing moves my mind from all the distractions that surround me, and my thoughts begin to align and finally my heart seeks the most important One. After a few minutes, I will begin to pray aloud. If you struggle with prayer, try the prayer journal. I pick up a box full of spiral-bound, lined paper journals during Back-to-School season every year.

Today, my prayers are significantly different than what I whispered in the early years of my marriage. Although I pray about the same things, the way I pray, the words I speak and my convictions have changed. And I'm convinced that the prayers I offer up today, move heaven in response.

I challenge you to create and stick to a time to read the Word and pray daily. Write out a prayer, asking the Lord to help you create a time and space for Him alone. God loves to honor this kind of prayer.

_____

_____

_____

_____

_____

_____

_____

_____

_____

_____

Turn in your book to the prayer titled, 'Psalm 139' by Jim Edwards. Personalize the prayer and then pray it aloud. Write today's date next to the prayer. pg 91

Essential components of effective prayer:

1. Create a time and space devoted to Bible reading and prayer

My friend, God intends to set His intercessors upon a broken, dark and evil world. As believers, we are empowered through the Holy Spirit to fulfill our generation's mandate to pray and bring His Kingdom to earth. Are you ready? Because I believe we sit upon the precipice of time to witness the fantastic.

Chapter Two
Praying The Word of God

By Lynn Donovan

Bless the LORD, you his angels, that excel in strength, that do his commandments, hearkening unto the voice of his word.
— Psalm 103:20 (NKJV)

The WORD.

In the beginning, God created the heavens and the earth. Now the earth was formless and empty, darkness was over the surface of the deep, and the Spirit of God was hovering over the waters. *And God said…*—Genesis 1:1-3

And God said.

My friend, in the first paragraph of the Bible we receive a powerful revelation. God spoke, and there was light. He spoke again, and the world was instantly created. It blows my mind to consider that the voice of God is *the* most powerful force in the universe and the heavenly realms. If we look further into scripture, we can read about Jesus and how He spoke supernatural healing, deliverance and correction to people. Further, still, the scriptures teach that as image bearers of God and joint-heirs with Christ (Romans 8:17), our words through faith and the indwelling of the Holy Spirit are filled with power.

- *The prayer of a righteous person is powerful and effective. — James 5:16*

- *The tongue has the power of life and death, and those who love it will eat its fruit. —Proverbs 18:21*

- *But I tell you that everyone will have to give account on the day of judgment for every empty word they have spoken. — Matthew 12:36*

- *There is one whose rash words are like sword thrusts, but the tongue of the wise brings healing.* — *Proverbs 12:18*

I wonder, do you want your prayers to be *words of the wise that brings healing*? I sure do. I've come to understand that our spoken words in prayer are indeed powerful, but they take on an extra dimension when we pray the Word of God. Praying in tandem with the Word has a direct correlation to what happens in the spiritual realm. I know this is true because of this verse:

> *Bless the LORD, you his angels, that excel in strength, that do his commandments, hearkening unto the voice of his word.*
> — *Psalm 103:20 (NKJV)*

When I speak the Word, the angelic respond. In Psalms 103:20 it tells us that angels hearken unto the voice of His Word. Hearken is defined as: *To give heed or attention to what is said; listen.* I'm convinced that praying the Word in conjunction with my requests moves angels into assignments of protection, provision and purpose. They are compelled by the repeating of the Word of God, which is spoken in faithful prayer by God's children.

Let me give you an example of how to pray using one passage from the Bible.

> *For you died, and your life is now hidden with Christ in God.*
> — *Colossians 3:3*

I pray aloud something like this:

Lord, today I am standing in faith for myself, my husband and my children. I declare to the spiritual realm that my husband, Mike, my daughter, Caitie, my son, Brad, my granddaughters and myself are all hidden with Christ. And Lord, I know we are hidden with Christ within You because that is what Your Word states in Colossians 3:3. Lord, right now we are hidden from the plans of the enemy. Right now, the enemy cannot see us, nor know where we are, nor where we are going today. The enemy cannot hear our conversation or make plans to harm us. The enemy cannot form any weapon against us, because we are hidden from their view in the natural and spiritual realms. We are completely at peace as we rest with Christ, in You, just as your Word promises. We are all hidden today from calamity, evil and defeat. We will prosper in all Your promises and walk in the gifts of the Spirit of Galatians 5. I pray all this and set the angels on assignment to harken unto Your Word as I speak it in faith through Jesus and the Holy Spirit. In Jesus' name. AMEN!

I often pray this passage in authority, as a child of God, for my family. Now, think this through. I am hidden. I'm *hidden* from *who*? Well, I hide myself and my family from the enemy, the demonic realm. And what gives this passage further power and strength is that I have a double portion of protection. I am not only hidden with Christ, but I'm hidden in God. Let me assure you that any ole' devil that wants to mess around with me or any of my family members will have to face an impregnable source of protection—that would be God and Christ Jesus. Wow! And finally, I believe that the angels who are sent to protect and serve me (Hebrews 1:14) are then set on missions and assignments, because I have prayed in faith and spoken God's Word.

This is only one example of praying the Word. I pray many passages for myself and family and much more over people I meet or the Lord sends to me for prayer. I pray passages online often in the comments on our blog or in blog posts. I believe fully that my words are spoken (or typed) in faith and that the spiritual realm is compelled to honor them. And you know what, very often I see the responses to my prayers later in the day. I always give thanks to my Father in heaven and I praise the name of Jesus. Hallelujah!

To pray the Word in faith begins in our quiet time. Pouring the Word into our hearts and memory banks, so that in the precise moment when we need God's truth and power to move in our lives in response to prayer, the Word springs from our lips and angels move!

Pick any scripture that is of importance to you in your current season. Personalize it and write a prayer below. Then pray it aloud in faith and know that angels hearken unto the Word of the Lord!

_____

_____

_____

_____

_____

_____

_____

_____

_____

_____

_____

Turn in your book to the prayer titled 'A Prayer for the Home and Family' by Dr. Christi Butler. Personalize the prayer and then pray it aloud. Write today's date next to the prayer. 93

Essential components of effective prayer:

1. Create a time and space devoted to Bible reading and prayer
2. Use the Word of God in your prayers

Chapter Three
Prayer Strategy: Belief
By Lynn Donovan

And without faith it is impossible to please God, because anyone who comes to him must believe that he exists and that he rewards those who earnestly seek him. — Hebrews 11:6

Of late, the Holy Spirit is shouting to my soul two words: Prayer Strategies. Truly, just ask Dineen. Every time I'm on the phone with her, prayer strategies are the topic of conversation. And wow wee, I am receiving some powerful prayer tactics for this season.

My friend, I'm grieved that for far too long the church has languished in powerless prayers. We simply aren't experiencing the breakthroughs that God is anxiously waiting to pour out. Well, NO LONGER! We are gaining knowledge about how to pray, and we will pray with a fierceness that sets the captives free and releases the prisoners from darkness. What say you? Ready for the next strategy?

Belief!

Simple really. But also utterly complicated.

And without faith it is impossible to please God, because anyone who comes to him must believe that he exists and that he rewards those who earnestly seek him. —Hebrews 11:6 (NIV)

A key component to effective prayer is belief. Really, belief is the core of all issues of faith. We simply MUST believe. What does that mean and what does that really look like? Good questions.

In the early years of my mismatched marriage, I struggled for a long time in my faith because I had a relationship with the church and not with Jesus. What I mean is that the primary focus of my time, learning and prayer life was centered in the church. I didn't study the Bible on my own, I only believed what I heard from the pulpit. I didn't pray much. My prayers consisted of sporadic utterances of crisis prayers. You know, the kind of prayers where you beg God to intervene when you have totally screwed up your life? Yep, I was a crisis-praying kinda girl. Good grief, so embarrassing to admit. But I'm guessing I'm not alone.

Because my faith was built on sand, I lacked the depth of relationship and Bible wisdom I needed to cease doubting and truly believe what God said about me and my life through His word. Praise be to God, because if you are truly hungry for more of Him, the Lord will go to great lengths to bring you into full faith.

We MUST believe in God, His Word, His plan and His purposes for us, our family, our community, our nation and the world. When you take that step over that line in the sand and vow to never look back in doubt, a whole new realm of answered prayer will begin to unfold.

Recently, I have come to fully believe what the Word teaches about healing. I have experienced supernatural healing. Read that story online at Spiritualyunequalmarriage.com, search for the title 'Does Jesus Heal Today.'

I've also prayed for others for their healing and have watched in astonishment, as Jesus touches people with emotional and physical healing. I have prayed healing over myself many times and it happens. Say what? I'm still mystified about how this all works, but I fully believe God heals, thus He does.

Here is a recent example where I prayed for myself. Yes, you can pray healing for yourself. In January 2016, a week after I returned home from a Spiritually Mismatched conference in Detroit, Michigan, I found myself dealing with a nasty eye infection in my right eye. It was goopy, icky, and not going away. Finally, as the week passed it became painful. I was using drops and some sort of ointment at night, all to no avail. The infection became worse. The pain was unbearable in the morning as I was sending my daughter off on her way back to college for the spring semester. After waving goodbye in the driveway in the bright morning sun, I stepped back into the shade of the garage and the stinging pain hit my eye like a 2x4 in the face.

Immediately I began speaking, quite loudly, in the middle of my open garage in the middle of my neighborhood a prayer of blessing. I prayed something like this:

In the name of Jesus, I bless my eye to be absolutely healed. This infection is not of God. Jesus, right now touch and heal it. I declare my eye is healed and whole. In Jesus' name. AMEN!

I prayed with passion and belief. I was so exasperated by the continued annoyance of it all, that my voice rose in passion in the middle of the garage. Upon the 'amen,' I walked into the house, through the laundry room, down the hall, and into the kitchen. I stood there for a minute thinking about what task to tackle next. Lost in thought, I absentmindedly reached up to rub my eye. And with a quick back and forth, I felt something on my hand. I lifted my finger to take a look and there on the tip was an old contact lens. It must have been there since the conference. Once it was removed, I was instantly healed.

I prayed in faith and was immediately healed. Hallelujah! Our God, our amazing Father, is so good and kind. Thank You, Lord!

My friend, we need to step into belief. Did you read the last half of the verse I shared earlier?

He rewards those who earnestly seek him.

Let's choose to believe. Really believe. How do we do this? Start to pray for supernatural faith. Say out loud that you believe the Word of God. And when a moment in time arrives, and you must make a choice between fear or faith, CHOOSE FAITH!

Okay, who needs to state clearly that they want to step into a new level of faith? Write out a new statement of belief below and then pray it aloud in Jesus' name.

_____

_____

_____

_____

_____

_____

_____

_____

_____

_____

_____

Turn in your book to the prayer titled 'Revelation of the Power in Your Love' by Joanne Marsh. Personalize the prayer and then pray it aloud. Write today's date next to the prayer. P 80

Essential components of effective prayer:

1. Create a time and space devoted to Bible reading and prayer
2. Use the Word of God in your prayers
3. Believe — Hebrews 11:6

Chapter Four

Prayer Strategy: Confidence

By Lynn Donovan

This is the confidence we have in approaching God: that if we ask anything according to his will, he hears us. — 1 John 5:14

Let's be the kind of believers that when our feet hit the floor each morning the devil says, "Oh crap! They're awake!"

Are you walking in belief today? You are becoming a prayer warrior that scares the crap out of the demonic. Wahooooo! So, let's work on another component of effective prayer.

Confidence.

Yep, and it's often a public thing. Confidence is crucial for effective prayer.

Confidence follows right on the heels of belief. It's the next step, no, it's the next BIG jump-off-the-cliff moment that you choose to believe and then follow through with confidence. Our Father greatly desires that we develop into people of Godly confidence.

Let me give you an example of what I think this looks like in real life.

My local church offers a once a month "Overflow Worship" night. We come together on a Sunday night and sing praise and worship songs. I LOVE overflow night. I experience some of the most profound and intimate encounters with the Lord through worship. About a year ago during one of these services, the worship leader paused the music and said, "Anyone who wants an extra touch tonight from the Lord, come on down to the front."

At first, no one moved. No one wanted to be the first. No one wanted all eyes on them. The people in the audience feared the reactions of those around them so much that it kept them from an opportunity to receive a touch from God. I can tell you there were people in the auditorium, who REALLY wanted to go forward. They ached for a chance that God would see and help them, but fear kept them pinned to their seat.

NOT this girl. I decided in that moment I didn't care what people thought. I wanted God more. I moved out of my seat and walked straight up to the front. Finally, a few more people joined me. But many remained seated.

This is what I believe God is looking for in His kids. He is waiting on the edge of His seat, hoping, cheering and urging our spirit to respond to Him. And it's often in the public square that God creates these moments to exercise our faith. He wants us to take a step of faith to receive His blessing, healing and more. He's speaking over us something like this, "Come on, baby girl. You can do this. Take one confident step out of the shadows, out of the fear. Show me you are willing to take a step for Me, and I will throw the floodgates of heaven open for you."

Love is a choice. We make hundreds of decisions every day and those choices are largely guided by love or fear. Choose love. God is calling His children to purposefully love. Choose to believe. Choose to be confident in what we know is true.

Confidence is a compelling quality in a believer.

By the way, do you know what I received because I stepped out of the shadows and went down front during the worship service? Well, I'm convinced I saw an angel that night. It's an astonishing story, but alas I'm way over word count for this chapter. *grin* I must share it another time.

Okay, now here is the rub. Because you just read this chapter on confidence, God is likely to place before you a moment where you are offered the opportunity to step out in faith and choose love. The "opportunity" is likely to arise within the next few days, and it's probable that you will be required to make a public display of faith. So, pray now so that you are ready. Then respond and watch the floodgates open!

Write a summary of your encounter below and read it often as a memorial (a memory stone) of what God is doing in your faith and prayer life.

Date:_____

_____

_____

_____

_____

_____

_____

_____

_____

_____

_____

_____

Turn in your book to the prayer titled 'I Assure You' by Patty Tower. Personalize the prayer and then pray it aloud. Write today's date next to the prayer. *Pg 81*

Essential components of effective prayer:

1. Create a time and space devoted to Bible reading and prayer
2. Use the Word of God in your prayers
3. Believe — Hebrews 11:6
4. Confidence

I pray you are filled with overflowing confidence and that your "courageous" encounter fills your heart and touches this world.

Chapter Five

Engaging Your Will

By Lynn Donovan

*Love the Lord your God with all your heart and with all your
soul and with all your mind and with all your strength.*
— Mark 12:30

The human *will.*

Our will. Our free will.

Free will is highly debated in the church today. For those of us
who are married to pre-believers, we understand the human will and
how it relates to faith better than most. Daily we pray and hope our
spouse will engage his/her will and turn to Jesus. But what many believers don't realize is that our will, when engaged in prayer, is incredibly
commanding.

Exercising our will is similar to engaging confidence and belief
in prayer. However, there is something more that lends power to our
prayers when our "free will" is purposely involved.

As Christians, Jesus instructed us to pray His will be done on
earth as it is in heaven (The Lord's Prayer – Matthew 6:9-13). Becoming
a powerful intercessor happens when God's will and our will are aligned
in truth, and we contend in prayer through strong conviction.

Employing our will beyond a shadow of a doubt, knowing that it
is the Lord's purpose to bring about the fulfillment of your prayers, will
move the Lord's heart and angels respond in kind.

The only way I can think to explain is to provide two examples.

One: *O Lord, I humbly ask that You would be kind to me. I have a
headache and it won't go away. Lord, if it is Your will, please heal me. Amen.*

Two: *In the name of Jesus Christ of Nazareth, I state clearly right now that Jesus died for my complete healing. I come before the Throne of Grace to be healed completely and permanently by the blood of Jesus. Holy Spirit, right now, in Jesus' name, I command this pain in my head to leave and never return. And in the place of pain, I speak peace, joy and healing. I praise You, Lord, for loving me so much that You were wounded, died and rose to life to complete my healing. I walk in Your love and healing right now. In Your powerful name, Jesus. AMEN!*

I wonder, do you discern the difference?

Do I believe God can and does respond to both prayers? Yes. However, my practice through years and thousands of prayers provide me with practical experience and knowledge that when believers pray within our authority, exerting our full conviction (our will) in belief and with confidence, the heavenly realms respond. First, angels move under this kind of direction, and second, demons flee as they are afraid of what you might say next. It scares the crap out of them.

When I pray and demand that the demonic leave someone for whom I'm praying or for myself, I go on to set the demons on fire and chain them in the pit, never to return. They don't want to mess with me, my friends. *grin* (Could it be that I am a small-but giant badass in the Kingdom? Can I say that in a Christian book? *wider grin*)

I have a question for you. Have you prayed in this manner, in full belief, with confidence and exerting your full will? Have you had someone pray over you who prays with these convictions? Below write down a prayer experience where you engaged your will. Or write out a prayer asking the Lord for revelation and instruction on how to apply your will to your prayers.

_____

_____

_____

_____

_____

_____

_____

_____

_____

_____

_____

Turn in your book to the prayer titled 'SALVATION' by Dineen Miller. Personalize the prayer and then pray it aloud. Write today's date next to the prayer. P. 71

Essential components of effective prayer:

1. Create a time and space devoted to Bible reading and prayer
2. Use the Word of God in your prayers
3. Believe — Hebrews 11:6
4. Confidence
5. Engage your will

Let's be a community of badasses for the Kingdom of God and start kicking butt and taking names and chaining the demonic in the pit! Woohoo!!!

You are an amazing prayer warrior!!!

Chapter Six
Courageous Intercessors
By Lynn Donovan

Fear not, for I am with you;
Be not dismayed, for I am your God.
I will strengthen you,
Yes, I will help you,
I will uphold you with My righteous right hand. — *Isaiah 41:10*

Do you believe God wants courageous kids?

I'm convinced that He does. Throughout the Bible, the Lord commands us to be courageous and to "fear not." It's easy to say, yet fear is difficult to defeat. What does living a life of courage look like in our modern era? Is it possible to pray without fear?

I'm convinced that the attributes we have studied so far in this book—praying the Word, belief, confidence, engaging your will—all lead up to courageous praying. Prayers that are spoken from the heart with just a tiny bit of courage, ROCK the heavens and defeat the demonic realms.

All the attributes we have considered thus far, lead us into the supernatural realm of unwavering faith, but courage lights our words on fire!

There comes a day when we overcome our doubt and truly believe. There is a moment in time when the Word of God comes alive, and we begin to wield a sharp, two-edged sword (Hebrews 4:12). There is a season in our lives after we have walked in step with Jesus where we become more than conquerors and grow into courageous, sold-out, Jesus-freaks. That is the moment where love conquers fear: fear of defeat, fear of man, fear of failure, fear of condemnation, guilt, shame and comparison. We finally step into the reality that we are a Child of THE Most High God and are empowered as Kingdom royalty. And thus, we experience the truth of Proverbs 18:21.

Death and life are in the power of the tongue,
And those who love it will eat its fruit. — Proverbs 18:21 (NIV)

My friends, when I grow up, I want to become this kind of believer. *grin*

When we arrive at this place in our faith walk, we become intercessors clothed in humility, men and women who are fully clad in supernatural power! We are believers who have spent time in the Presence, in the secret place, alone with God. We are warriors who know the Word and how to pray it, and when the Word is aptly spoken, it's as beautiful as baskets of fruit of silver and gold (Proverbs 25:11).

I know there are "big name" believers in our Christian communities such as Beth Moore, Tony Evans and others who are powerful intercessors. However, what impresses my heart more than big names is the ordinary mom who rises early to pray for her little ones by name. I'm moved by the dad who prays every day on his way to work for his family and for the Kingdom of God to be advanced in his workplace. I'm undone to consider the ordinary widow who is alone at home and at the utterance of her small voice, literally thousands of angels are sent on assignment to save this world and shape culture.

Oh, how I want to be one of THESE believers. I want to pray and see people healed emotionally and physically. I want to pray and watch as America — all the nations of the world — return to God and serve Him with abandon. I want to pray and bear witness that those who are tormented by fear and illness are set free. I'm moved to pray and know that the name of Jesus is glorified in all the earth.

My friend, we are the church and we are headed toward this purpose. God chose us to learn, in this season, to pray with power and to bear witness to the salvation of our families. We are the chosen to bring love, forgiveness, healing and hope to many through our prayers.

So, right now all you need to do is declare this: I BELIEVE. And now pray aloud with me:

I believe in God our Father.

I believe in Christ the Son.
I believe in the Holy Spirit.
I believe I can pray with power.
I believe I can utter words and angels move.
I believe that I was born for such a time as this to bring the Kingdom of God into its rightful place in our world.
I believe God listens and loves to answer my prayers, even the outlandish stuff.
I believe I am commissioned to be an intercessor, a prayer warrior and a powerful servant of the Most High.
Today, I will pray with purpose, power and belief, using the Word with conviction, confidence and finally with unfailing courage. I will not relent or give up or give in. I will stand for goodness, honesty, integrity, and truth. I will love lavishly and forgive easily. I will offer hope and a hand to those who I can help, and I will always and forever remain loyally in love with my Jesus.
This is my high and holy calling, and I will believe nothing less. In the name of Jesus. Amen and Hallelujah!!!

Stand tall because your prayers are bringing His Kingdom to earth. Can I get an amen? Write a courageous-outlandish-prayer-dream-hope-request below. And pray with courage for yourself and your family, as well as the others in our community. Woo Hoo!

_____

_____

_____

_____

_____

_____

_____

_____

_____

Turn in your book to the prayer titled 'Binding the Strong Man' by Flavia A. Personalize the prayer and then pray it aloud. Write today's date next to the prayer. *P 8 3*

Essential components of effective prayer:

1. Create a time and space devoted to Bible reading and prayer
2. Use the Word of God in your prayers
3. Believe — Hebrews 11:6
4. Confidence
5. Engage your will
6. Courage

My Prayer: I pray for every nation to come to the truth that Jesus is the son of God, and through Him, they have the abundant life now and for all eternity. I approach the Throne of Grace with confidence and boldness to contend for the full salvation of my husband and family members. I pray that the fire of the Holy Spirit falls on me with such intensity that I can pray for others and they are healed, delivered and receive a powerful encounter with the Father's love. I pray for everyone who reads this prayer that they see the goodness of the Lord in the land of the living (Psalm 23:13). In Jesus' name. AMEN!

Chapter Seven
Breaking Principalities
By Lynn Donovan

For we wrestle not against flesh and blood, but against princi-
palities, against powers, against the rulers of the darkness of this
world, against spiritual wickedness in high places.
— *Ephesians 6:12 (NKJV)*

I've shared with you six prayer strategies that I absolutely believe magnify our prayers and they are moved upon by the Lord. And as I was considering wrapping up teaching on strategies, the Lord reminded me about a position of prayer that I've yet to discuss: Fasting.

There are times when we have prayed and prayed, employed our will, the Word, etc., etc. And . . . nothing. Why?

Well, let's take a look at the utterly astonishing account of unanswered prayer in the book of Daniel. Chapter 10. Let's listen in on this conversation:

Daniel's account, starting with verse nine (NLT): *Then I heard the man speak, and when I heard the sound of his voice, I fainted and lay there with my face to the ground.*

Just then a hand touched me and lifted me, still trembling, to my hands and knees. And the man (Gabriel, whom I had seen in the earlier vision) said to me: "Daniel, you are very precious to God, so listen carefully to what I have to say to you. Stand up, for I have been sent to you." When he said this to me, I stood up, still trembling.

Then he said, "Don't be afraid, Daniel. Since the first day you began to pray for understanding and to humble yourself before your God, your request has been heard in heaven."

There are so many things about this exchange that blow my mind, but I want to point out something that most of us miss when reading this passage. Notice that it says *"since the first day you began to pray."* What is amazing, beautiful and loving is that God heard Daniel on the very first day...

And even better, God sent an answer immediately.

My friends, I'm fully convinced that this is still true today. God listens and wants to answer immediately. But here in this passage in the book of Daniel is where things become very interesting.

Answers are delayed. Answered prayer can be thwarted by our own words and can be amended if we change our prayer or God has another plan in motion. But in my heart I'm convinced that His love and goodness moves Him to reply with immediate answers to our heartfelt prayers.

Let's listen to the rest of this astonishing conversation between Daniel and the angel Gabriel.

Gabriel, Verse 12: *"I have come in answer to your prayer. But for twenty-one days the spirit prince of the kingdom of Persia blocked my way. Then Michael, one of the archangels, came to help me, and I left him there with the spirit prince of the kingdom of Persia. Now I am here to explain what will happen to your people in the future, for this vision concerns a time yet to come."*

WHOA!

God replied to Daniel immediately but the answer was met with an epic battle in the spiritual realm that went on for 21 days! My friend, this passage is in the Bible in order that we may also understand how prayer and answers to prayer unfold. We must recognize that contending in relentless prayer is often needed. Prayer with fasting is needed to break a block in the spiritual realm. Daniel fasted the entire 21 days awaiting an answer that he was certain would arrive.

We could spend months on the study of prayer with fasting, but we won't as we cover fasting every January during our powerful community fast. Join us the first week, every January for our annual fast at spirituallyunequalmarriage.com

When you fast with the intention, seeking the Father's heart, to hear His voice clearly, your prayers combined with fasting facilitates an answer so commanding that it can break through powerful principalities of the dark realm.

Wow and WOW!!!

I wonder if you have sensed that you were battling in prayer on the spiritual plane, against a strong darkness, right before a breakthrough? Things that make you go, hmmm. I would love to hear your stories of effective prayer and fasting. Contact me through the website and share your breakthroughs.

I know the discipline of prayer with fasting can be a confusing area for those who have never fasted. So, plan to join us in January as we fast together. We always cover various types of fasting and prayer at that time. Or visit the website and search: Fasting.

I love you deeply, my friends. I'm praying for our community, and I'm expecting breakthroughs!

If there are areas of breakthrough and need in your life that you have been praying over and have yet to see answers arrive, write these prayer needs below. Write out a prayer that you are contending for these answers, and that you're committed to seeing breakthrough and answers from our heavenly Father. Consider a daytime fast to accompany this prayer.

Date: _____

_____

_____

_____

_____

_____

_____

_____

_____

_____

Turn in your book to the prayer titled 'Your Promises' by H. Brough. Personalize the prayer and then pray it aloud. Write today's date next to the prayer. *P 89*

Essential components of effective prayer:

1. Create a time and space devoted to Bible reading and prayer
2. Use the Word of God in your prayers
3. Believe — Hebrews 11:6
4. Confidence
5. Engage your will
6. Courage
7. Fasting

Chapter Eight
Praying Our Power Passage
By Lynn Donovan

For the unbelieving husband has been sanctified through his wife, and the unbelieving wife has been sanctified through her believing husband. Otherwise, your children would be unclean, but as it is, they are holy. — 1 Corinthians 7:14

My friend, there are many more aspects of prayer that we could cover. We won't cover everything in this book, but I have shared with you what I sense the Lord is desiring to impart to the church in this season to teach us to pray with power in the Holy Spirit.

Today, I want to speak to one more area that is highly specific to those who are unequally yoked. And in just a couple of more chapters, we'll uncover the "blocks" to prayer and how to process unanswered prayers.

About a year ago I was wrapped up in a personal study focused on spiritual warfare. Because I'm married to a pre-believer, the warfare in which I engage is frequent in my home and feels at times, relentless. So, I began reading, listening and gleaning from many sources about how to experience triumph in my prayers. I wanted victory through my prayers to facilitate peace in my home and make my house a place where the Holy Spirit dwells. Do you want that as well?

Okay, so I learned a ton. But as I studied one morning, I nearly fell out of my chair when I discovered a power-passage specific to those of us who are married to unbelievers.

First, let me state that the spiritual realm is governed by laws. These are spiritual procedures and regulations that were instituted by God. Just as in the natural, for example, there is the law of gravity. Well, in the spiritual realm there are laws the angelic and demonic must abide by and they are meticulously followed. The demons search relentlessly for any possible way to gain access into our lives through laws that are violated. A violation occurs when we believe a lie about God or about who we are in Christ. A violation opens an opportunity for the enemy to gain access to our lives.

So, why am I giving you a lesson in spiritual laws? Because we must understand how authority works. There is a structure to authority in the spiritual realm. God has ultimate authority. The Bible teaches us that God has given all authority to Christ. We, as joint heirs with Christ, receive authority in some manner or degree. We access that authority through our faith and prayers. All this to say: The structure of the family is a system of authority that is ordained by God. The Bible teaches us that the husband has authority over his wife (Ephesians 5:23). And thus, parents have authority over their children.

Why does this matter? Because men who are Christians can pray for protection over his wife and children and the demonic realm MUST listen. But in our mismatched marriages, our spouse is not under the authority of Christ so we could be left vulnerable. But . . . we are not.

This is the secret the demonic does not want you to know. We are empowered in a spectacular way to pray protection, favor, blessing and much more over our unbelieving spouse through 1 Corinthians 7:14.

For the unbelieving husband has been sanctified through his wife, and the unbelieving wife has been sanctified through her believing husband. Otherwise, your children would be unclean, but as it is, they are holy. - 1 Corinthians 7:14

THIS IS OUR VERSE OF POWER AND AUTHORITY.

And let me tell you I use this passage often. And I see results.

My friend, this truth is our authority to pray away things that are not of God in our spouse's life and over our children. The rules of familial authority in this passage apply to the spiritual realm. I don't know how to explain this well other than to just pray and show you how I use this passage in my prayers for my home and family.

Often, almost daily, I will pray something like this:

In the name of Jesus, I take authority over my home through the power of the Word of God in 1 Corinthians 7:14. I stand in faith over my home and declare it is now holy as stated in this verse. My husband is now covered with the holiness of Christ and covered by His blood. My children are holy, and they will walk in the glorious plans and purposes designed for them since before time began and declared by God. My children, husband and I will experience the abundance of the Lord today in our schools, ministry, workplace and anywhere and everywhere we go.

I say that any unclean spirit that is in my house MUST go right now into the pit. (I will name any here as the Holy Spirit leads me. The demonic gains access to my home at times through the television my husband watches at night.) Lord, in Jesus' name and by the authority as the believing spouse, I command all demonic spirits of fear, pride, unbelief, political spirit, religious spirit, etc. to leave right now. I state clearly that they cannot come back, nor can replacement spirits come in. I bless my husband to receive the love of God through me and all darkness is forbidden to be in my home. In Jesus' name.

Father, I take authority over my children through 1 Corinthians 7:14 as their mother. I say they are blessed and will receive today every spiritual gift you have prepared for them. They will experience Your joy, peace, and goodness (Romans 14:17) as this is Your loving and lavish provision for them. And Lord, as I speak this blessing over them, I claim it for myself and my husband. In Jesus' name.

Thank you, Lord, for the angels that You have stationed around and in my house. I stand with them in Your power and authority through Jesus as the protector and guardian against evil. I declare today my family and home are safe zones and nothing unclean can enter in. I declare today that blessings, peace, and grace rest here in the power of the Holy Spirit and Jesus Christ. I stand with my armor fully on and in faith under the truth of 1 Corinthians 7:14. In the powerful name of Jesus Christ my Lord. AMEN! Hallelujah!!!

Okay, do you need some authority in your home? Well, now you have it. Say this prayer out loud and write your version of it below. *We love You, Jesus. Thank You.*

_____

_____

_____

_____

_____

_____

_____

_____

_____

_____

_____

Turn in your book to the prayer titled 'Sprinkle Clean Water Upon My Wife' by Ian Acheson. Personalize the prayer and then pray it aloud. Write today's date next to the prayer. P. 110

Essential components of effective prayer:

1. Create a time and space devoted to Bible reading and prayer
2. Use the Word of God in your prayers
3. Believe — Hebrews 11:6
4. Confidence
5. Engage your will
6. Courage
7. Fasting
8. Pray our power-passage: 1 Corinthians 7:14

Let's release the Kingdom of God into our family line and sanctify our home, spouse and children. AMEN…

Chapter Nine
Prayer Strategies
For Your Heart

By Lynn Donovan

Give thanks in all circumstances; for this is God's will for you in Christ Jesus. — *1 Thessalonians 5:18*

I am excited about sharing a few thoughts about how to process unanswered prayer, but before we get to that, we must turn our consideration toward two key prayer strategies which bridge us to breakthroughs.

Worship and Thanksgiving.

My friend, sometimes our prayers morph into a laundry list. We pray over our to-do lists bringing names and circumstances before our King that are truly significant and needful of prayer covering. However, there are seasons where we can become caught up in our pain, needs and daily concerns and our prayers will become inwardly focused. We can lose our perspective. When we discover ourselves in this rut, it's imperative that we refocus and be reminded that we aren't just praying. We are engaged in a life-long, love conversation with our Father, with our Bridegroom-Prince, Jesus and the Holy Spirit.

The Lord truly knows our needs and yes, I believe we must pray and speak our concerns to His heart. But take a minute and imagine our Papa God, waiting, hoping even longing for us to approach the Throne of Grace and just hang out. Be intentional to lean in to listen to Him and then ask the Lord about what He's doing. What is He doing on earth today? Let's inquire about what thrills His heart and what makes

Him smile. My friend, let's be thoughtful to turn our affection toward our Lord and our Father. Let's be deliberate about our love by offering spontaneous worship and thanksgiving through our prayer time and all throughout the day.

Specifically, my prayer time begins with praying with what I call my "three thankfuls." I write in my prayer journal, Three Thankfuls and the date. Then I scribble out the first three things that come to my mind and simply acknowledge that everything good in my life comes from my Papa.

Recently I heard a pastor teaching on this aspect of intimacy in prayer. He said that he rarely brings a list before the Lord but instead brings his affection. He said something like this, "God already knows my heart and my needs. So I am intentional to bring my affection to Him. And He usually moves on my heart requests."

Interesting.

I believe there is a time to petition, and there is also time to just be (Psalm 46:10)! It's wisdom and discernment fueled by relationship that takes us perfectly into each.

So for this chapter, I have another challenge for you. When you lay down to go to sleep, rest quietly and turn your affection toward the Lord. In your imagination or quiet prayers, give Him your heart and then let Him love on you. I will bet you will enjoy some fantastic nights of restful, joyful sleep! Zzzzzzzzzz!

Write out your three "thankfuls" and turn your affection toward Him:

_____

_____

_____

_____

_____

_____

_____

_____

_____

_____

I love you my friend! You LOVE well. You love God, and you love people. Well done, good and faithful servant!

Turn in your book to the prayer titled 'Bless My Husband' by Heather Passuello. Personalize the prayer and then pray it aloud. Write today's date next to the prayer. **P /24**

Essential components of effective prayer:

1. Create a time and space devoted to Bible reading and prayer
2. Use the Word of God in your prayers
3. Believe — Hebrews 11:6
4. Confidence
5. Engage your will
6. Courage
7. Fasting
8. Pray our power-passage: 1 Corinthians 7:14
9. Thankfulness and worship

Chapter Ten
Why Isn't My Spouse Saved Already? Unanswered Prayer

By Lynn Donovan

The Lord is not slow in keeping his promise, as some understand slowness. Instead he is patient with you, not wanting anyone to perish, but everyone to come to repentance. — 2 Peter 3:9

We have covered many aspects of creating a powerful prayer life. Now I want to chat about what to do with our confusion and disappointment when our prayers remain unanswered. And specifically, why isn't my spouse saved?

As I mentioned, my husband and I have been together for more than 25 years. I have prayed, pleaded, bargained, begged and everything and anything in between to convince God to save my husband. And save him yesterday already.

Anyone else in this place with me??? Anyone???

Well, there are a few things to bring before the Lord when you are praying and not receiving an answer. We first must ask, "Am I praying within the will of God?"

This is an easy question and one that is also difficult. When it comes to God's will to save our spouse, the Word is clear.

The Lord is not slow in keeping his promise, as some understand slowness. Instead he is patient with you, not wanting anyone to perish, but everyone to come to repentance. — 2 Peter 3:9

So, you gotta wonder, if I'm praying with sincerity with a heart full of love and hope and within the will of my Father, WHY IN THE WORLD ISN'T THIS MAN SAVED?

Yep, I know I'm not alone in asking this question.

Here are my thoughts. I believe the Word and *I am* praying in faith and conviction using my will. Thus God sends me to this statement in His Word:

The jailer called for lights, rushed in and fell trembling before Paul and Silas. He then brought them out and asked, "Sirs, what must I do to be saved?" They replied, "Believe in the Lord Jesus, and you will be saved—you and your household." —Acts 16:29-31

My friends, I believe that my husband will be saved. My husband has already been sanctified (made holy) because of my faith in Jesus. If you read our book, *Winning Him Without Words*, you will remember I shared the account of my husband praying the prayer of salvation with Joe on our driveway.

I watched it happen. I listened to him speak the words. It has been accomplished. I will live believing that God will honor His Word and that my husband will find his way to heaven. However, right now my reality is that my husband is not living for Jesus.

Yes, I'm bummed out about it. My husband is missing out on an amazing life God had prepared for him. God has stored up for my husband rich blessings, wonder, adventure and peace. Our marriage has missed out on a great deal as well because of our faith differences. These are sacrifices I have laid down on the altar of love for my Savior.

I know that you are also laying down many of your hopes and dreams for your marriage. But, let me be the voice of hope and state that all we have laid down, God will pour back into our lives in good measure, pressed down, shaken together and running over (Luke 6:38). In this life and throughout all eternity.

What is difficult is that God's timing is not our timing. God's ways are not our ways (Isaiah 55:8-9). And we struggle to surrender our expectations and timelines to God's sovereign plan. Sometimes I think the best prayer we can pray for our spouse's salvation is this:

Lord, have Your way with me. I surrender all my expectations and limitations. Fill me with Your wisdom and revelation. Place contentment within my spirit and supernatural love in my heart. Let me turn my eyes fully to You and believe without a doubt that You have the utmost best and greatest plans and intentions for my life, family, and marriage. I trust You and will live intentionally to draw near to Thee. In Jesus' name. AMEN!

Today, let's become "lay-down lovers of Jesus." Let's turn our face fully toward Him and allow His love to fill our hearts and trust Him to fulfill His Word toward our spouse and children.

Below, write your spouse's name, children's names and follow it by 1 Corinthians 7:14 & Acts 16:29 as a statement of faith. I'll start us out.

Mike, Caitie, Brad and granddaughters — 1 Corinthians 7:14 & Acts 16:29. They are sanctified and saved. It is written. I believe. It is done. In Jesus' name. AMEN!

_____

_____

_____

_____

_____

_____

_____

_____

_____

_____

I love you, my friends. I hope one day to see the people whose names you have written standing with us before the Throne of Grace, for all eternity.

Turn in your book to the prayer titled 'On These Promises' by Dee Rusnak. Personalize the prayer and then pray it aloud. Write today's date next to the prayer. P. 108

Essential components of effective prayer:
1. Create a time and space devoted to Bible reading and prayer
2. Use the Word of God in your prayers
3. Believe — Hebrews 11:6
4. Confidence
5. Engage your will
6. Courage
7. Fasting
8. Pray our power-passage: 1 Corinthians 7:14
9. Thankfulness and worship
10. Perseverance

Chapter Eleven
What Blocks Answers To Prayer?

By Lynn Donovan

*I had cherished sin in my heart, the Lord would not
have listened —Psalms 66:18*

Many things can actually block prayer. Our own words can snatch our prayers right out of the spiritual realm. That's one way our prayers become blocked. And there are several others. Let's take a look at what schemes the enemy employs to blow up our prayers.

Our love for our God leads us to ask the same question that King David asked. We don't ask out of guilt or condemnation. We ask because we want to know if there is anything that is keeping us from experiencing "more" of the Kingdom.

Deliberate, willful and habitual sin creates a disconnect in our prayer life. In the Word, rebellion is as bad as witchcraft (1 Samuel 15:23). There is a time in our faith walk where we come to a place to ask the Lord, *"See if there is any offensive way in me, and lead me in the way everlasting."* —Psalms 139:24

When I'm walking in faith, the Lord will often point out areas in my life that are stealing parts of my soul away from righteousness (His goodness and blessings). The Holy Spirit will clench my heart over things in the moment. Certain television shows that I once watched are no longer a good thing for my heart and mind. God will reveal certain friendships or relationships that are toxic and draining to my joy. There are seasons of growth where the Holy Spirit is persistent to caution me to listen and then turn away. These moments often arise in a split second of decision. I can say quickly, "Naw, it's not that big of a deal." Or make other excuses like, "I can handle this. It's not scary or too violent or over sexed or against Biblical values."

These moments of ordinary small decisions happen every single day. We can either follow the Holy Spirit or our flesh. When we choose the Spirit over and over, God then releases you into a higher level of love, authority, and power, and your prayers are moved upon by angelic forces.

My intention is not to throw you into condemnation (Romans 8:1). God's mercy and faithful-forgiveness cover our every failure. We need only ask. I'm convinced the Lord is cheering for us. He looks upon our lives and speaks with the love of a Father, "Baby girl (My son), I know how very difficult it is. I knew before I sent you to earth that you would face enormous difficulties and pain. I knew you would screw up your life. I KNOW it's very, very hard down there. I just want you to do the best you can and learn to love Me first and then others. It will all be okay. Just do your best."

My friends, rest in His love. If He's asking you to give something up, it's because it's to make room in your life for more of His love and goodness, His gifts and promises. Let Him reign!!!

I'm leaving this place for you to write an earnest prayer of confession/repentance that leads to your freedom and increased areas of powerful prayer. You can also talk to the Lord about issues, thoughts and habits He is calling you to surrender.

_____

_____

_____

_____

_____

_____

_____

_____

_____

_____

Turn in your book to the prayer titled 'Clothe My Husband in Tenderhearted Mercy' by Taylor Talmage. Personalize the prayer and then pray it aloud. Write today's date next to the prayer. P. 76

Essential components of effective prayer:
1. Create a time and space devoted to Bible reading and prayer
2. Use the Word of God in your prayers
3. Believe — Hebrews 11:6
4. Confidence
5. Engage your will
6. Courage
7. Fasting
8. Pray our power-passage: 1 Corinthians 7:14
9. Thankfulness and worship
10. Perseverance
11. Repentance

Chapter Twelve
Our Expectations And Answers To Prayer

By Lynn Donovan

For my thoughts are not your thoughts, neither are your ways my ways," declares the Lord. "As the heavens are higher than the earth, so are my ways higher than your ways and my thoughts than your thoughts. —Isaiah 55:8-9

I have an astonishing story to share with you about how our prayers can remain unanswered or when answers are delayed. This story explains that often our expectations are not quite what the Lord has in mind for our lives. Let me take you to a very old passage.

Now the gates of Jericho were securely barred because of the Israelites. No one went out and no one came in.

Then the Lord said to Joshua, "See, I have delivered Jericho into your hands, along with its king and its fighting men. March around the city once with all the armed men. Do this for six days. Have seven priests carry trumpets of rams' horns in front of the ark. On the seventh day, march around the city seven times, with the priests blowing the trumpets. When you hear them sound a long blast on the trumpets, have the whole army give a loud shout; then the wall of the city will collapse and the army will go up, everyone straight in." — Joshua 6 :1-5

Don't let the familiarity of this story steal the outrageousness of what happens here. God tells the Israelites to do something seemingly ridiculous. I mean absolutely absurd. Can you imagine an army launching an offensive against a city and instead of piling up dirt and stones to scale the walls, instead of practicing warfare and battle tactics, God instructs them to march around the enemy?

And get this. On the seventh day, God instructed the Israelites to march in silence.

Say what?

The Israeli battle tactic appears, stupid! At least in the eyes of men. Ah, but that is what is so cool with God. When God moves, you know with certainty that it is His hand at work. We can experience the same certainty in our prayer life.

It's a known fact, that we, the spiritually mismatched, have a creative imagination. We have specific expectations of how we think God should move in our spouse's life to bring about his/her salvation. We have conceived of every idea that is possible to help convince our spouse to choose faith in Jesus. Often in our prayers, we freely supply God with much-needed advice and suggestions as to how He might go about making our dreams come true. Anyone?

Yikes. Okay, I admit this was true of me in years past.

However, after many years of praying, dwelling in His Presence and receiving answers from the Lord, I've learned He RARELY answers my prayers in the manner I expect. Typically, His answers are always slow. He seldom answers within the circumstances I imagined or hoped, or according to my timeline. However, when the Lord moves, it's always amazing and the results are fantastic—exceeding my expectations so much so that all I can do is take in His glory. He answers larger than it's possible for me to dream. And I can dream up some pretty big stuff.

God may ask us to believe and follow up on our faith with actions, covered with courage and conviction that feels absurd in the moment. And in response to this kind of unshakable faith, He is likely to show up with absolutely unexpected and miraculous provision. The story of the Walls of Jericho is a historic reference for us today. The defeat of Jericho is ridiculously outlandish and therefore we know that falling walls is at the hand of God. Hallelujah!

My friend, prayer is at the core, a conversation between two "in love" hearts. Prayer is devotion and time together. It's a relationship of consideration, respect, honor, and peace. It's love and friendship. It's worship and teaching. It's a Father and His child, for whom He made a tremendous sacrifice to bring into His life forever.

It's my heart's cry for you today that your prayer life is enriched. I pray you witness and participate in the astonishing answers that can only be by the hand of God. I pray that you watch as walls are torn down and lives are changed because you prayed. My hope is that you bear witness to supernatural healing and that your spouse falls to his or her knees in surrender to Jesus the Christ. I pray with conviction and belief that you will experience the goodness of the Lord in the land of the living and that your life is forever changed because you prayed with outrageous faith. In Jesus' name. AMEN!

Write out a prayer of outrageous hope below. Date it and then trust the Lord. Take a look at this prayer and all the others a year from now. Let the Lord dazzle you with His love, mercy, kindness, favor, healing and freedom. In Jesus' name. AMEN!

_____

_____

_____

_____

_____

_____

_____

_____

_____

_____

Turn in your book to the prayer titled 'By Faith and Not Sight' by Flavia A. Personalize the prayer and then pray it aloud. Write today's date next to the prayer. P 107

Essential components of effective prayer:

1. Create a time and space devoted to Bible reading and prayer
2. Use the Word of God in your prayers
3. Believe — Hebrews 11:6
4. Confidence
5. Engage your will
6. Courage
7. Fasting
8. Pray our power-passage: 1 Corinthians 7:14
9. Thankfulness and worship
10. Perseverance
11. Repentance
12. Pray expectantly

I love you, my friends. Pray in the power of the Holy Spirit… And change the world for the cause of Christ!

Chapter Thirteen
The Release

By Lynn Donovan

Peace I leave with you; my peace I give you. I do not give to you
as the world gives. Do not let your hearts be troubled and do not
be afraid. —John 14:27

As we conclude this study, I want to give you a gift. The gift of peace.

In John, chapter 14, it's apparent that Jesus' followers are deeply troubled and fearful. What is beautiful about this entire chapter is that Jesus speaks peace over them, a heavenly peace that is different than the world.

Isn't it true that as believers today, we also find ourselves troubled and fearful over many things? Specifically, we are troubled over our loved one's salvation decision. For many of us, we unknowingly place on our shoulders the entire responsibility to bring our spouse to faith. This burden feels like we're wearing a suffocating, burlap sack of exhaustion.

I've prayed for more than 25 years for my husband's salvation. I've fought the good fight. I've contended for his heart, soul, mind, will and emotions on every battle front that I could think to pray. I've thrown into the trash, piles of wet tissues as I would cry and pray, cry and pray. I have stormed the heavenly realms in defense of my faith and home and warred with tremendous evil that has left my spirit battle scarred.

Recently I realized that throughout all the praying and warring, I was becoming obsessive about my husband's salvation and my prayer-focus turned further toward my enemy. I focused less upon my good Father. My prayers became obsessive and perhaps the demonic gained a toe-hold which allowed my prayer life to become somewhat oppressive.

Somehow I lost clear sight that Jesus loved my husband more than me, and He was fully capable of responding to my prayers of faith.

I know that contending in prayer, faith and in the fight for our spouse and children is necessary. And I believe that we must pray in seasons that are assigned to us by the Lord, as situations change and as prompted by the Holy Spirit. However, there comes a day where we unknowingly step into weariness.

It is the perfect will of our good Father that His children live in joy, peace and goodness (Romans 14:17). Looking back over the past several months of my prayer life, it was obvious that I was anything but peaceful. This realization hit me like a ton of bricks recently while in a prayer session with Dr. Charles Kraft, whom I greatly respect. After explaining my prayer focus upon my husband's salvation, he looked gently into my eyes and said, "Pray and release."

Wow, pray and then release my husband into the hands of my Father. In that moment, I felt as though that heavy burlap sack lifted off over my head and disappeared into thin air. Peace came rolling in like a flood! Woo Hoo! It was awesome and I still feel that way today! Hallelujah!

My friend, the Lord didn't design us to carry ridiculous burdens. And something as noble as praying and contending for the salvation of our spouse can morph into a heavy load we were never designed to carry.

> Jesus said, "Come to me, all you who are weary and burdened, and I will give you rest. Take my yoke upon you and learn from me, for I am gentle and humble in heart, and you will find rest for your souls. For my yoke is easy and my burden is light."
> —Matthew 11:28-30

This verse is our rescue from weariness! This passage frees us to take His yoke—not our unequally yoked marriage—upon us. He is gentle, humble and we will find rest.

Peace.

Let's pray for our spouse and then RELEASE him or her into the loving arms of Jesus Christ. Right now, Jesus is calling you to choose. Choose peace. Choose love. Choose to pray and then release it all to the King of peace. All that He requires is our worship and thanks.

As we remain in Him and as life moves along, we will be called upon to war again in prayer for our loved ones, but until that time, walk in peace.

Do you know what I believe is the most influential thing we can do as believers to impact the lives of our families? Simply live the abundant life of John 10:10. Let's live life every day, in all our circumstances, filled with peace, joy, hope, excitement and adventure in Jesus Christ. And let love be our highest calling in all that we do and say. This is the kind of faith-life that changes hearts, heals homes, honors our Lord and brings hope to our world.

Thank you for taking this journey with me. I have been praying for you the whole way through. I am called by the Lord to share these prayer strategies because GREAT things are ahead for earth because we pray. Thank you for loving our Jesus, your spouse and family. Thank you for being a Kingdom warrior for the cause of Christ Jesus.

Love, Lynn.

Write your prayer of release.

_____

_____

_____

_____

_____

_____

_____

_____

_____

_____

Essential components of effective prayer:

1. Create a time and space devoted to Bible reading and prayer
2. Use the Word of God in your prayers
3. Believe — Hebrews 11:6
4. Confidence
5. Engage your will
6. Courage
7. Fasting
8. Pray our power-passage: 1 Corinthians 7:14
9. Thankfulness and worship
10. Perseverance
11. Repentance
12. Pray expectantly
13. Pray and release

It is for freedom that Christ has set us free. Stand firm, then, and do not let yourselves be burdened again by a yoke of slavery.
— Galatians 5:1

Part II:
Salvation Prayers
& Spiritual Warfare
Strategies

SALVATION: J*An i7 /i7*
God's Revealed Word
for the Spiritually Mismatched

By Dineen Miller

One morning I began asking God for specific words and/or impressions from Him for my family. My favorite verse to pray as I do this is Jeremiah 33:3. As I listened for His heart, I heard a very clear word and realized this was not just for me, but a corporate word for all who are spiritually mismatched.

That word was SALVATION. And the accompanying Scripture was Jeremiah 24:7:

I will give them a heart to know that I am the Lord, and they shall be my people and I will be their God, for they shall return to me with their whole heart. — Jeremiah 24:7 (ESV)

Praying for Figs

As I prayed for understanding and wisdom as to what this word means, the Holy Spirit continued to lead me back to Jeremiah, a very challenging book to read in the Bible. But thankfully His intentions became clear as I reached chapter 24:

After King Nebuchadnezzar of Babylon exiled Jehoiachin son of Jehoiakim, king of Judah, to Babylon along with the officials of Judah and all the craftsmen and artisans, the Lord gave me this vision. I saw two baskets of figs placed in front of the Lord's Temple in Jerusalem. One basket was filled with fresh, ripe figs, while the other was filled with bad figs that were too rotten to eat.

Then the Lord said to me, "What do you see, Jeremiah?"

I replied, "Figs, some very good and some very bad, too rotten to eat."

Then the Lord gave me this message: "This is what the Lord, the God of Israel, says: The good figs represent the exiles I sent from Judah to the land of the Babylonians. I will watch over and care for them, and I will bring them back here again. I will build them up and not tear them down. I will plant them and not uproot them. I will give them hearts that recognize me as the Lord. They will be my people, and I will be their God, for they will return to me wholeheartedly. — *Jeremiah 24:1-7 (NLT)*

The Holy Spirit impressed upon me that our pre-believers are like the good figs, and then He showed me how we are to pray for them in connection to our word, salvation. I believe that our mission is to "plump" up our pre-believers with our love, the love of Jesus. And our challenge is to determine (make the choice) to walk in faith that God's will and purpose for our pre-believers will be done.

Praying for Peace and Prosperity

Then the Holy Spirit revealed more of God's heart for our pre-believers through Scriptures in Jeremiah. More specific than I anticipated, so I asked Him to please confirm that I was hearing Him correctly.

That Sunday morning, the pastor of my church spoke on the EXACT same Scriptures and message that the Holy Spirit had shown me for our pre-believers. I can only imagine what I looked like as I sat there with my eyes bugging out and my mouth hanging open.

Simply put, part of God's message for us is Jeremiah 29:11, a verse we know very well. But He showed me what He was asking us to do as we wait for the salvation of our pre-believers.

"Build houses and settle down; plant gardens and eat what they produce. Marry and have sons and daughters; find wives for your sons and give your daughters in marriage, so that they too may have sons and daughters. Increase in number there; do not decrease. Also, seek the peace and prosperity of the city to which I have carried you into exile. Pray to the Lord for it, because if it prospers, you too will prosper." — *Jeremiah 29:5-7*

The Lord was instructing the Israelites through Jeremiah to thrive and prosper in the place they were in. Let me be clear that the Holy Spirit isn't saying that we have been exiled in our marriages. And also let me clarify, that if you read Jeremiah in its entirety you will see that God instructed them to do this in order that they may live and not die. His plan most likely made little sense to them from a human perspective—to go into exile as captives to another country, yet God's plan was for them to grow, thrive and prosper.

Our circumstances do not often reveal the plans and purposes of God, but they will reveal His presence at work if we seek Him and seek to obey what He is asking us to do in that moment or place in our timeline.

> *"For I know the plans I have for you," declares the Lord, "plans to prosper you and not to harm you, plans to give you hope and a future. Then you will call on me and come and pray to me, and I will listen to you. You will seek me and find me when you seek me with all your heart." — Jeremiah 29:11-13*

And God spoke this to my heart: "Steward well what I have given you."

The Promise of His Covenant

The rest of God's message for us is in Jeremiah 33. Here are the key verses, but I encourage you to read the entire chapter and seek the Lord to bring this promise into your heart and home.

> *Then this city* (our homes) *will bring me joy, glory, and honor before all the nations of the earth! The people of the world will see all the good I do for my people, and they will tremble with awe at the peace and prosperity I provide for them.*
> *— Jeremiah 33:9 (NLT)*

> *The joyful voices of bridegrooms and brides will be heard again, along with the joyous songs of people bringing thanksgiving offerings to the Lord. They will sing, 'Give thanks to the Lord of Heaven's Armies, for the Lord is good. His faithful love endures forever!' For I will restore the prosperity of this land to what it was in the past, says the Lord. — Jeremiah 33:11 (NLT)*

> *And this will be its name: 'The Lord Is Our Righteousness.'*
> *— Jeremiah 33:16 (NLT) (Prophetic reference to 2 Cor. 5:21: We are the righteousness of God in Christ Jesus)*

> *"This is what the Lord says: If you can break my covenant with the day and the night so that one does not follow the other, only*

then will my covenant with my servant David be broken. Only
then will he no longer have a descendant to reign on his throne.
The same is true for my covenant with the Levitical priests who
minister before me." — Jeremiah 33:20-21 (NLT)
(The covenant with David was the prophetic word and promise
of Jesus coming.)

My friend, as I read this part, the Holy Spirit whispered John 3:16 to my heart. We know this verse well...

For God loved the world so much that he gave his one and only
Son, so that everyone who believes in him will not perish but
have eternal life. God sent his Son into the world not to judge the
world, but to save the world through him. — John 3:16-17 (NLT)

And this is God's reassurance that He will do what He has said. I hear God speaking this to us right now, that He is faithful and nothing will stop or hinder the promise He has given us.

But this is what the Lord says: "I would no more reject my
people than I would change my laws that govern night and day,
earth and sky. I will never abandon the descendants of Jacob or
David, my servant, or change the plan that David's descendants
will rule the descendants of Abraham, Isaac, and Jacob. Instead,
I will restore them to their land and have mercy on them."
— Jeremiah 33:25-26 (NLT)

This is a powerful promise. Jesus is the final covenant. Our God is not slow to answer our prayers for our pre-believers (2 Peter 3:9). He's just setting things up for the right time so the revelation of His covenant (Jesus) to our pre-believers would be so full that they would turn to Him with their entire hearts (wholehearted!), just as He said in Jeremiah 24:7.

I will give them hearts that recognize me as the Lord. They will
be my people, and I will be their God, for they will return to me
wholeheartedly. — Jeremiah 24:7 (NLT)

I know without a doubt that our God is at work in our marriages, and we will begin to see a great harvest among our pre-believers. I have walked this path of the mismatched for more than 20 years and have prayed as faithfully as possible, each prayer that God has given me to pray for my husband. And now I am beginning to see the harvest of the seeds I have planted. Even others are noticing this shift.

So, my dear friend, let's not give up when we are on the verge of such a stunning breakthrough. The Lord is asking us to seek the peace and prosperity of our marriages in a whole new way. And the key is love. To love with the heart and passion of Jesus Christ flowing through us. That is what I have witnessed to be most powerful in my marriage, and I am now convinced it is foundational to thriving and planting seeds in our marriages, to transformation and salvation!

I believe with my whole heart that time is now. It's our harvest time! Hallelujah and Praise Jesus! Amen!

Prayer: *Lord, I come before You in great humility, recommitting my marriage to You. I stand ready to steward well my marriage and my family as You are calling me to do. I trust You, Lord, to provide all that I need to do this and to inspire me with great knowledge and wisdom to love my pre-believer with the love of Jesus. Today I declare that my marriage will be a place of peace and prosperity for the glory of Jesus Christ.*

Lord Jesus, set Your eyes on (spouse's name) for good. Bring him/her to the land of faith. Build him/her up and plant him/her with deep roots. Give him/her a heart to know You are the Lord. Fill me with Your love in great abundance so that I can pour that love into (spouse's name) so he/she will be as a plump fig for Your harvest.

Lord, thank You for giving (spouse's name) a heart that recognizes You as the Lord. I declare that (spouse's name) will be Your people and You will be his/her God, for he/she shall return and turn to You with his/her whole heart. In the Mighty name of Jesus, amen!

About Dineen Miller

Dineen is passionate about God's Word and truth. She's been featured on the Moody Radio Network, Focus on the Family Radio, Dr. James Dobson's FamilyTalk, FamilyLife Today and INSIGHT on Miracle Channel. She is the coauthor of the award-winning book, *Winning Him Without Words* and *Not Alone: Trusting God to Raise Godly Kids in a Spiritually Mismatched Home.* She is also the author of the ACFW Carol Award winning book, *The Soul Saver.* She and her husband love to collect shells and walk the famous white sands of Siesta Key Beach,

Florida. Visit Dineen online at SpirituallyUnequalMarriage.com and DineenMiller.com.

Jan 25/17

Clothe My Husband In Tenderhearted Mercy

By Taylor Talmage

Let my husband put away all bitterness, rage, anger, harsh words and all evil behavior. Allow him to be kind, tenderhearted and forgiving of others, just as God has forgiven him (Ephesians 4:31-32). Prevent anger from controlling my husband. Do not let the sun go down on his anger, do not give the devil this opportunity (Ephesians 4:26-27).

Lord, help him strive for peace with everyone and to work at living a holy life, for if he is holy, he will see the Lord. Guide me as I look after my husband so that he will not fail to see the grace of God. Do not let a root of bitterness trouble my husband (Hebrews 12:14-15). Help my husband love his enemies. I pray that he will not persecute others and that others will not persecute him once he becomes a man of God (Matthew 5:44-45).

Clothe my husband with tenderhearted mercy, kindness, humility, gentleness and patience. Help him make allowance for other's faults and forgive those who offend him. Lord, You have forgiven my husband, help him to find the peace that comes with the forgiveness of others (Colossians 3:12-13). If someone continuously offends him, help him to continuously forgive (Luke 17:4).

Lord, bless my husband with all of these things, as he has been forgiven through Christ Jesus (1 John 2:12). Father God, calm my husband's hurt and restless heart. Bring peace and love to our home during troubled times. Help my husband to let his guard down and discover the freedom in Jesus that he so desperately needs.

About Taylor Talmage

My name is Taylor, and I am the mother of two beautiful children and the wife of a man who is going to be blown away the day that he embraces the unfailing love of Jesus. I am a daughter of the King, striving to live by the Word, so that the world will know that God loves them even as He loved His one and only Son. Taylor lives with her family in Kansas.

Three Little Words

By Evie Vandergrifft

I became a Christian at age 28, seven years after a wedding ceremony that was devoid of all references to God and holiness. I wish I could say my prayers have always been consistent as I wait for my husband's salvation, but I can't. My prayers for him have ebbed and flowed like the tides. Twenty-one years of waiting, and sometimes I just don't have the heart or energy to pray for him to be saved. It becomes a silent prayer with only his name and that feeling of longing. God knows. Must I utter it again?

In truth, it wasn't only my frequency or focus of prayer that was inconsistent. The motivation behind my prayers also drifted. I wanted my husband to taste and see the beauty and goodness of the Lord because I loved him AND Jesus. As time wore on and I struggled to raise two boys into Christian men alone, my prayers remained the same, but the heart behind them didn't. Add a third child, caring for my dying parents and the stresses of life, my motives insidiously slipped into selfishness. Like many of us, I created this ideal of marriage in my mind. If my husband would only become a Christian and assume his role as spiritual head of the household, all of this would be so much easier! I imagined him powerfully praying over me and that I could openly pray for him. We would pray for our children together, have family devotions . . . you know the story.

But after twenty-one years I no longer wait on my husband. I have learned to wait only on the Lord and look to Him expectantly. The motivation behind my prayers for my husband and his salvation are out of love and for his benefit alone. I don't want him to miss out on the best and most important thing in life, a relationship with Jesus Christ. I have been forgiven, healed, refined and tested many times over. I can say with confidence God always arrives. Just not in the ways you may think. Three little words turned our lives around.

I remember the exact day I was led to pray, "Make him hungry." *Led* is too gentle a word. I was compelled to pray them. Choir practice was wrapping up and the choir leader was asking for prayer requests. Usually, I remain silent, but this night, silence wasn't an option. I asked the choir to pray those three words. God, "Make him hungry." Truly, I had no idea the boldness of this prayer!

At the time one of our sons was graduating from high school and the other was a year behind him. Our boys would be leaving soon. Our daughter was in the first grade with barely a sprig of a pigtail and a toothless smile. Time with her was like a picnic on a summer day, sweet and uncomplicated. I couldn't help but grieve that my husband was missing all of it! His career had eclipsed all else.

"Just one more promotion and we will be set," he would assure me.

The boundary line between work and our lives was completely blurred. Often, he arrived home late and tired just to work some more.

"Lord, he's missing it." That was the context for those three little words.

My husband really is a great guy. He is warm, generous, and a loving husband and father. I am incredibly proud of him. He was the first in his family to earn a four-year college degree. He has worked for the same corporation since graduation and has climbed his way up. He is a man of integrity. He truly cares about the people who work for him and with him. He really is one of the good guys.

That is what made what happened next so painful. Just weeks after praying those three little words, "make him hungry," the company to which he'd devoted 24 years of service, turned on him. Actually, the company turned on us.

Accusations were made against him regarding favoritism and inappropriate behavior with a female employee. "Ouch!" There was an internal investigation, of which I will spare the details. The allegations were based on hearsay. The investigation revealed that he was innocent.

However, to be thorough, they felt justified to interview everyone that has ever worked with him. It went on for months. The Salem witch trials came to mind.

They interviewed everyone, male and female, to inquire if my husband had ever done anything inappropriate or made any comments that made anyone feel uncomfortable. Even though he was found innocent, his reputation was tarnished forever by the inquiry and insinuations alone.

Despite our spiritual differences, my husband and I have a great relationship. I absolutely believe he is incapable of such duplicity nor would he have the energy or need. Imagine if our marriage was strained when this occurred? It wasn't. I am so grateful that God kept me grounded. My heart ached for my husband. I knew his identity was in his job, and he viewed his co-workers as his friends. He felt rejected and betrayed.

Interestingly, the Lord had recently led me to a season where a hidden idol fell and fell hard. And because of my experience, I could comfort my husband. It opened the door for conversations about trusting in Christ alone for identity, worth and value.

My husband hasn't come to faith in Jesus yet, but he did return to us. God took something meant for evil and used it for good. Our marriage is stronger than it has ever been. When he is home, he is present. We just spent six days on a beach together and his computer never left his bag.

Three little words, "Make him hungry." A simple prayer led by the spirit, motivated by love and answered by a powerful, faithful God.

About Evie Vandergrifft

I live in Houston, TX where I am an adjunct biology professor and serve in women's ministry. My passion is to teach and write things that encourage believers to live like Christians and to represent Him well. I am the author of The Delight Project (thedelightproject.com), an online community that seeks transformation through delighting in God, feeling His delight in you and delighting in others.

Revelation of ~~Jan 16/17~~
the Power in Your Love

By Joanne Marsh

THANK YOU, Father, for revelation of the Power in Your Love!

I repent of going against Your Word, Lord God, that warned me not to become unequally yoked in marriage.

I thank You for teaching me that by activating Your Word, I will see change.

In marriage, I became one with_____, and by Your Word and in my Salvation, I became one with You also.

With childlike faith as I walk in the Spirit now, I am living with one foot in the Kingdom. And in the Kingdom, 1 + 1 = 3 of us walking together.

Thank You, Lord Jesus, that as I love You, Your Love flows through my heart into my spouse. Only Your Love can fill the void.

I surrender all my expectations for_____now. By Your strength and Spirit in me, I will seek You with all my heart, so that Your agape love can flow freely through me into_____, causing the change I could never create on my own.

I pray this out loud in Jesus' name, because the words I speak are Spirit, and they are Life.

Glory to You, Lord!

Amen!

John 6:63

Am I missing something? That was my thought when I realized the Truth wasn't setting me free.

And so, as Solomon asked for wisdom, I did too and, O MY WORD, God delivered! My life has been stirred up since a teacher hand-picked by my Father entered my journey and a deeper understanding of God's wisdom and Word changed my course! I am blessed to be able to listen to this teacher for hours each day and, by doing so, I have experienced a deeper hunger, an awakening of revelation knowledge in my Father's Living Word coming to life and an understanding beyond words of God's heart for us.

God's heart is the key to effortless change in our lives. I finally realized by letting go of this life and simply surrendering to His will and by keeping a Kingdom perspective in my life rather than an earthly view, my heart was changed supernaturally. The power of His love began to flow. THAT I learned by watching Lynn Donovan activate this very action at the Spiritually Mismatched Conference in Detroit, Michigan, at the beginning of 2016.

I have personally witnessed and experienced His compassion in this same way, touching me and moving through my heart to connect with others on my path. It is an incredibly humbling experience. He planted a seed within my heart years ago to change the world.

One person at a time.

Now…it's my husband's turn to experience God's love through me! Let Your Kingdom come! Amen!

About Joanne Marsh

I am Joanne Marsh, a child of the Most High God, and I am madly in love with my spiritually-equal Groom who thrills me each day with unique experiences of His Love. All it took was total surrender and a very inquisitive heart to experience the spirit realm. Joanne lives with her husband in Ontario, Canada.

I Assure You *Jan 17/17*

By Patty Tower

Not long after my salvation, I felt a burning desire in my heart for my husband to know the Lord. Let me explain, my husband is not a lukewarm sort of guy. I know this to be true because he has made snide references and smirks regarding "hypocritical" Christians. And refuses to be tied to a belief system where people are supposed to live according to the Bible, but then live contrary to its teaching. If he is going to believe in someone like Jesus, it will be all or nothing. His passion is one of the many qualities I adore about him.

Following my salvation, my unbelieving spouse suddenly seemed distant from me. The Lord began to gift me with a new set of eyes to see and ears to hear differently than before. Therefore, we butted heads on many topics, such as sex before marriage, cohabitation, or certain medical interventions. On top of praying fervently, I wrote and wrote in my journal, begging God for an answer on "when." I made a decision to not ask "**whether** his salvation would come," or "**if** it will come," thinking these words would indicate a lack of faith.

About a year into my prayers and writing, I attended a Jesus encounter event. One of the intercessors at the event walked over to me to ask if I had a prayer request. My reply, "Yes! My husband to come to the Lord." She then explained to me that she prayed a Scripture over her husband and one year later, to the day, her husband was saved. Hallelujah! Her testimony was the assurance and answer I was waiting to hear. The Scripture is from 2 Timothy 2:25-26:

> *He must correct his opponents with courtesy and gentleness, in the hope that God may grant that they will repent and come to know the Truth [that they will perceive and recognize and become accurately acquainted with and acknowledge it], And that they may come to their senses [and] escape out of the snare of the devil, having been held captive by him, [henceforth] to do His [God's] will. (AMP)*

Two years have passed since then, and my faith in God's promise has not wavered. I continue to pray and fast, pray and fast. Words have been released for our future marriage ministry and our heart for God. Words and visions have flowed to me regarding the two of us spreading the gospel, not only in America but also around the world. Recently, a sister in Christ gave me a vision of my husband weeping at his salvation. On the same night, God gifted me a dream, confirming her vision. When I needed the assurance, God has never failed. Remember John 16:23-24:

> *I **assure** you: Anything you ask the Father in My name, He will give you. Until now you have asked for nothing in My name. Ask and you will receive, so that your joy may be complete. (HCSB)*

These two years have been nothing but blessings and transformation on my behalf. I sense in my spirit that the closer my relationship with God grows, the sooner my husband's time will come.

About Patty Tower

Patty Tower lives in Seattle, Washington with her beautiful husband and son. She is praying and thanking God because soon her unbelieving spouse will surrender his heart to Jesus! She is an aspiring writer and blogger of www.pattytower.com. She dreams God will lead her to minister to thousands of women, who love Christ as much as she does.

Binding the Strong Man   Jan 17/17
by Flavia A.

Abba Father, I thank and praise You for all the blessings in my life. I thank You for my husband. I thank You for bringing us together and showering us with Your love.

Father, I surrender myself, my husband, my marriage and family to You. Let Your perfect will alone be done in our lives. Let Your kingdom come in my marriage. Fill us with Your Holy Spirit to lead and guide us each day of our lives.

I cover myself, my husband, my marriage, family, our finances, jobs and all our belongings with the precious Blood of Jesus Christ. I pray for a hedge of protection over and around us.

I cancel every wicked plan of the enemy against us in the mighty name of Jesus and through His precious Blood.

As Your Word says, "The angel of the LORD encamps all around those who fear Him, and delivers them." I release Your angels to protect and minister to us. Protect us from anger, temptation and addiction.

Lord, bless my husband. Help him to excel at his work. Open his eyes to see You and his ears to hear You. Surround him with Your good counsel and lead him on the right path.

Lord, Your Word says, "Believe in the Lord Jesus Christ and you will be saved. You and your household." I stand on this Word for my husband's salvation. Lord, call him to You and draw him closer to You. Reveal Yourself to him in a mighty and a powerful way.

Protect his mind from every lie, deception, false teaching, philosophy and worldly thinking. I break and destroy every demonic stronghold in his mind, in Your mighty name, Lord Jesus.

I bind his mind to the mind of Christ.

Lord Jesus, help me to be an excellent wife. Teach me to love my husband unconditionally just as You have loved him. Help me to understand him and be compassionate toward him. Fill me with Your wisdom and discernment to speak the right words to him.

Father, be the center of our relationship. Fill our hearts with Your love, joy, and peace. Surround us with Godly people, filled with Your Holy Spirit and wisdom.

Your Word says, "Behold, I give you the authority to trample on serpents and scorpions, and over all the power of the enemy, and nothing shall by any means hurt you." Lord Jesus, I take authority in Your name and bind the strongman of Anti-Christ. I break and destroy its power over me, my husband and my marriage, in the mighty name of Jesus. I break and destroy every spirit associated with the strongman of Anti-Christ in the mighty name of Jesus and through the precious blood of Jesus.

I bind and cast out the strongman of Deception working against me, my husband and my marriage, in the mighty name of Jesus. I bind and cast out the spirit of religion, false doctrine, lies and every spirit associated with the strongman of Deception in the mighty name of Jesus and through the precious blood of Jesus.

I bind the strongman of Fear. I break and destroy its power over me, my husband and my marriage, in the mighty name of Jesus. I break and destroy the spirit of anxiety, stress, fear of man and every spirit associated with the strongman of Fear in the mighty name of Jesus and through the precious blood of Jesus.

I bind the strongman of Bondage. I break and destroy its power over me, my husband and my marriage, in the mighty name of Jesus. I break and destroy the spirit of addiction, control, manipulation, religious mind control and every spirit associated with the strongman of Bondage in the mighty name of Jesus and through the precious blood of Jesus.

I bind the strongman of Jealousy. I break and destroy its power over me, my husband and my marriage, in the mighty name of Jesus. I break and destroy the spirit of division, unforgiveness, anger and every spirit associated with the strongman of Jealousy in the mighty name of Jesus and through the precious blood of Jesus.

Father, Your Word says, "No weapon formed against me shall prosper and every tongue that rises against me in judgment, You shall condemn." I stand on this Word and cancel every negative word spoken over myself, my husband and my marriage in the mighty name of Jesus and through the precious blood of Jesus.

I thank You, Father, for already giving us the victory through the shed blood of Your Son, Jesus Christ. I claim Your victory over my life, my husband's life and our marriage. I thank You and glorify Your Name. I ask all this in the mighty name of Jesus. Amen!

About Flavia A.

Flavia is an avid believer in the power of prayer. She and her husband have been married for two years. She lives in India with her husband. She is eternally thankful to God for all His marvelous works in her life.

Part III:
Praying the Word

Your Promises JAn 18/17

By H. Brough

O Lord, I call to You; come quickly to me. Hear my voice when I call to You. Thank You, Lord, that You will answer me and tell me great and unsearchable things I do not know. May my prayer be set before You like incense; may the lifting up of my hands be like the evening sacrifice. Let the morning bring me word of Your unfailing love, for I have put my trust in You. Show me the way I should go; unto You, I lift up my soul. Rescue me from my enemies, O Lord, for I hide myself in You. Teach me to do Your will, for You are my God; may Your good Spirit lead me on level ground. Search me, O God, and know my heart; test me and know my anxious thoughts. See if there is any offensive way in me, and lead me and (husband's name or 'my family') in the way everlasting.

Set a guard over my mouth, O Lord; keep watch over the door of my lips. Let my and _____'s hearts not be drawn to what is evil. I continue to ask You to fill us with the knowledge of Your will through all spiritual wisdom and understanding. And I pray that we may live a life worthy of You Lord, and we may please You in every way. I pray that You will open _____'s eyes and turn him from darkness to light, and from the power of satan to God, so that they may receive forgiveness of sins and a place among those who are sanctified by faith in You. I pray that _____will repent and turn to You, Lord, and prove his repentance by his deeds. For You have rescued each of us from the dominion of darkness and brought us into the kingdom of the Son You love, in whom we have redemption, the forgiveness of sins. Our Lord Jesus Christ, the glorious Father, give_____and me the Spirit of wisdom and revelation, so that we may know You better. I pray that the eyes of our hearts may be enlightened in order that _____and I may know the hope to which You have called us, the riches of His glorious inheritance in the saints. I pray that_____will live by the Spirit, and will not gratify the desires of the sinful nature.

Lord, fill_____and me with the fruit of the Spirit which is love, joy, peace, patience, kindness, goodness, faithfulness, gentleness and self-control. I pray that_____and I may be delivered from wicked and evil men, for not everyone has faith. But Lord, You are faithful and You will strengthen and protect us from the evil one. Please put the full armor of God upon us so that when the moment of evil comes, we may be able to stand our ground, and after we have done everything to stand, let us stand firm with the belt of truth buckled around our waists, with the breastplate of righteousness in place and our feet fitted with the readiness that comes from the gospel of peace. In addition to all this, let us take up the shield of faith with which we can extinguish all the flaming arrows of the evil one. Give us the helmet of salvation and the sword of the Spirit, which is the word of God. And let us pray in the Spirit on all occasions with all kinds of prayers and requests. With this in mind, let us be alert and always keep on praying for all the saints.

I praise You, Lord, that You will cleanse_____and me from all our impurities and from all our idols. You will give each of us a new heart and put a new spirit in us; You will remove from us our heart of stone and give us a heart of flesh. Thank You, Lord, that I am not afraid or discouraged because of this vast problem. For the battle is not mine but Yours. Thank You, Lord, that I can do everything through You who gives me strength. And You will meet all my needs according to Your glorious riches in Christ Jesus.

Thank You, Lord, for Your promises that what You have said You will bring about; what You have planned, You will do. Thank You for Your Word that goes out from Your mouth: It will not return to You empty but will accomplish what You desire and achieve the purpose for which You sent it. Our help comes from the Lord, the Maker of heaven and earth. For nothing is impossible with God. Thank You, Lord, for healing and restoring my marriage and for all marriages around the world. Father, all of these things I ask in the holiest name of Jesus Christ, Your Son. Thank You for hearing my prayer. You are everything to me. I love You, I worship You, I thank You and I trust in You. Amen!

About H. Brough

This prayer is a compilation of Scriptures that's been passed from sister to sister over the years. H. Brough lives in California with her husband and two children. Many people planted seeds of faith within her over her lifetime, and they eventually sprouted after she married and her children were born. She is thankful to know, love and share Jesus with her children and has faith that one day her husband will know Him also.

Psalm 139 *JAn 16, 2017*

By Jim Edwards

Dare I look into Your eyes, King Jesus?

One look and I know You have seen right through me—right through all my pretenses, and pretensions. You see everything I do—nothing can be hidden from You. And yet my eyes are drawn back to Your deep, deep wells of love, and to let You see into the very depths of who and what I am. Thank You that You don't violate my privacy and the privacy of my internal world.

Thank You, Lord, that there's no guilt or shame in Your look of love for me, no disappointment or hurt as You see and understand my thoughts and my heart. Thank You that I sense only a love that draws me to You and yearns for You to come and search out my heart, my motives, my longings, my loves. Oh, come and bring Your love, and Your wholeness to the broken places, Your peace to the fractured, and Your Joy to my heart.

Lord—I give You all my ways, I want to open all my heart to You—as if I really could hide anything anyway. For You know what I'm about to say before I've even formed the words. You formed and shaped me with such a loving touch from Your hand—Lord, the magnitude and detail of Your loving care is incredible—it's far too big for me to get my head around.

Where can I hide from You and the Holy Spirit? I'm having a hard job thinking why I would want to right now, but there are times when I'm hurt and angry and lashing out. If I go and take a ride in the International Space Station, You'll still be there with me, and I seem to remember that You made quite an impact on those who went to the moon. If I drop down in some underwater capsule to the depths and darkness of the Pacific Ocean, I won't have left You behind. Similarly, if I jet off into the sunrise and set up home on some distant island, that gentle tender touch of Your loving hand will never be far away, and Your right hand will never let go.

If I think to myself that surely some black-out curtains can turn the day into night, and You'll never be able to see me, then even when I can't see my own finger in front of my face—it will still be as bright as day to You.

Oh, my King Jesus—how did You create me in my mother's womb? You really are amazing—how You formed each part of my anatomy so uniquely, and my soul and spirit too. Even identical twins have such unique souls and spirits—they're still totally unique to You. Just how do You do that, Lord? Oh, everything You do is so wonderful—that has to be pretty obvious to everyone with eyes to see! All Praise and Glory to You!

Thank You that I wasn't an accident and hidden from You as I was coming together, but rather You had Your creative hand of genius putting me together totally in secret. You saw those cells growing and multiplying and already You had all my days written in the Lamb's book of Life—Wow!

Oh, Papa God, Your thoughts for me—they're so precious, so good, so big! And so numerous I could never count them if I tried—way more than the grains of sand on every seashore… When I stop my dreaming and wake up—oh—oh thank You my King—You're still with me and thinking of me.

Oh, that my thoughts were like that, Lord. You know the blood-thirsty, selfish, angry, proud thoughts that assail my mind inside, like my enemies outside who despise Your name "Jesus." Oh, You know how I hate them both, Lord. You know how I am so easily ensnared and seduced by their train of thought, and entertain them far longer than I should. Oh, how I hate them, and how they pollute my thought life. Lord search me. Lord come in and walk with me through every aspect of my heart and life. Lord, I want You to know me, to know me better than I know myself. I want You to show me anything that displeases You—anything Lord.

Lord, I can't change me—but You can change me. So Holy Spirit—show me and help me tend the garden of my heart with Your royal care. Help me to spot and weed out the weeds, the lies, the dishonesty, pride and fear. And help me to watch over and care for those shoots of lovingkindness, of wisdom, of humility, of hope, of faith and trust in You and of Your Love—Your special Agape, selfless kind of love. And help me to grow my heart to steward more of You, Holy Spirit—to grow in maturity and favor with those around me, and especially with You, Lord.

About Jim Edwards

Jim Edwards is a passionate lover of Jesus, living on the South Coast of the United Kingdom with his wife Val. They have been married more than 40 years and have four adult children. Jim is currently transitioning from his career as an Electronics Applications Engineer to author, self-publisher, and speaker. His prayer is an excerpt from *Living and Breathing the Psalms*, his third published book available through Amazon. Jim's heart is to peel back the church's layers of religious baggage, in order to reveal the mighty, powerful life and heart-changing love of Jesus in fresh ways through fresh language for today's believer.

A Prayer for the Home and Family
By Dr. Christi Butler JAn 16/17

Dear Heavenly Father, in the name of Jesus, I come boldly before Your throne today on behalf of my home and my family. I pray that You would wash me and cleanse me in the precious blood of Jesus and hear my prayers and give ear to my supplications (Ps. 143:1). I pray that these prayers would be set before You as incense and the lifting up of my hands like the evening sacrifice (Ps. 141:1). I pray that as I intercede on behalf of my family, You would be gracious to me, You would bless me, and You would cause Your face to shine upon me and my household (Ps. 67:1).

As I begin today, I wish to pray for Your grace and protection over my home and family. I believe that in the realm of the spirit, the weapons of our warfare are not carnal, but are mighty in God for the pulling down of every stronghold (2 Cor. 10:4), and I believe that the blood of Jesus is one of the mightiest weapons we possess, because it is written in Revelation 12:11, "And they overcame him [satan], by the blood of the Lamb and by the word of their testimony."

Therefore, I take the blood of Jesus in the realm of the spirit, and I apply it to my home, to my family, to my marriage, to all my family members, to my property, my pets, my finances, my health and all that concerns me. Just like the Israelites in Egypt took the blood of a lamb and applied it to the doorposts and everyone within their house was protected from the death angel that passed through the land (Ex. 12), so too, I take the blood of Jesus and apply it spiritually to my household and to everyone in it. Just like Rehab, the harlot, hung the scarlet cord in her window and everyone within her household was protected (Josh 2:18), so too, I lift up this standard of the blood, and I believe the blood of Jesus covers my home and my family in their coming in and in their going out.

I say, in the name of Jesus, no weapon that is formed against me or my household shall prosper and every tongue that rises up against us in judgment shall be shown to be in the wrong (Is. 54:17). I take authority over every assignment of satan to steal, kill, or destroy (John 10:10), and I forbid the enemy to harm my family or my loved ones in any way. Matthew 18:18 says, "Assuredly, I say to You, whatever You bind on earth will be bound in heaven, and whatever you loose on earth will be loosed in heaven." Therefore, in the name of Jesus, I bind the enemy and every demonic force assigned against me, and I loose the angels of God to accompany, defend and preserve me, and to bear me and my household up in their hands lest we dash our foot against a stone.

Because, it is written in Psalms 91: 11-12, "For He shall give His angels charge over you, to keep you in all your ways. In their hands, they shall bear you up, lest you dash your foot against a stone." You have also said in Your Word that the angels of God are ministering spirits sent to minister to those who will inherit salvation (Heb. 1:14), and that the angels harken to the voice of Your Word to perform it (Ps. 103:20). Therefore, send your angels to minister to my loved ones and to protect us in all of our ways, in our coming in and in our going out.

Furthermore, Heavenly Father, I confess and believe that You are a shield around us (Prov. 30:5), and You set a hedge of protection around us just like you set around Job (Job 1:10). I believe, according to Psalms 91:1, that my whole family shall be hidden in the secret place of the Most High, totally invisible and inaccessible to the enemy. Cause my household to be hidden with Christ, in God (Col. 3:3). And, I will say of the Lord, "You are my refuge and my fortress; My God, in You I will trust (Ps. 91:2)." I pray, according to Psalms 91, that You would deliver us from every snare of the enemy, from every sickness and from every evil plot. I declare that no evil shall be able to come near my home or my family (Ps. 91:3, 10). Instead, I believe that we will tread upon serpents and scorpions and over all the power of the enemy, and nothing shall by any means harm us (Luke 10:19).

I believe the Lord gives His angels charge over us and these angels encamp around us because we love and fear the Lord (Ps. 34:7). For You, God are my refuge and my strength, an ever-present help in trouble (Ps. 46:1). And, I believe and confess that my help is in the name of the LORD, who made heaven and earth (Ps. 124:8).

Therefore, I will rejoice in my God and my enemies shall turn back, fall, and perish at Your presence (Ps. 9:3). You, Lord, will go before us, and You will also be our rear guard. For You have promised in Proverbs 11:21 that the posterity (or the offspring of the righteous) will be saved, delivered and rescued from every evil attack. For You, O Lord, are a shield for me, my glory and the One who lifts up my head (Ps. 3:3).

Therefore, we will be strong in the Lord and in the power of Your might. We will put on the full armor of God, and we will stand firm against the devil and his schemes. We will stand and having done all, we will continue to stand (Eph. 6:10-18). Furthermore, we will be faithful to pray in the spirit on all occasions with all kinds of prayers and requests, and we believe You will hear and answer our prayers (Eph. 6:18). Cause our ways to be pleasing in Your sight and make our enemies to live at peace with us (Prov. 16:7).

According to Isaiah 49:25, contend with those who contend with us and intervene to save my children from every plot of the enemy. I pray that everyone in my household would continually submit themselves to God and that they would resist the devil and the devil will flee far from them. I pray that they would draw near to God, and You would also draw near to them in return (James 4:8). I pray that my household would cleanse their hands and purify their hearts from every sin and cease from being double-minded. Instead, cause them to have a heart that follows hard after you (James 4:8). Cause every member of my household to throw off everything that hinders and the sin that so easily entangles, and help us all to run with perseverance the race marked out for us, fixing our eyes on Jesus, the Author and Finisher of our faith (Heb. 12:1-2).

According to Ps. 51:10, I pray that You would create in all of us a clean heart and renew a steadfast spirit within us. Cause us to faithfully serve You all the days of our lives. I pray that we would no longer be conformed to the pattern of this world, but we would be transformed by the renewing of our minds (Rom. 12:2). And finally, I pray according to 3 John 2 that my household would prosper in all things and be in health, just as their souls prosper. Cause their souls to prosper and cause their light to so shine before men, that everyone would see the good works performed by those in my family and glorify the Father in heaven (Matt. 5:16).

As far as the salvation of my household is concerned, I confess and believe that You (God) will give everyone in my household a heart to know You. They will be Your people and You will be their God (Jer. 24:7). I declare in faith that as for me and my house, we will serve the Lord (Josh. 24:15). We will serve the Lord, and Your voice we will obey (Josh 24:24). My household shall call on the name of the Lord, and they shall be saved (Acts 16:31; Joel 2:12).

Father, You have said in 2 Peter 3:9 that You are not slack concerning Your promise as some count slackness, but You are longsuffering toward us, not willing that any should perish but that all should come to repentance. You have also said in 1 John 5:14-15 that if we ask anything according to Your will, You hear us. And, if we know that You hear us, we can know that we have the petitions we have asked of You. Therefore, I thank You in advance for the salvation of my household and my children.

I know that You hear me and the prayers of a righteous man or woman of God avail much (James 5:16). I believe that You are the God of the Breakthrough, and You are working miracles behind the scenes to bring my family to the saving knowledge of Christ. In a spirit of faith, I call every unsaved loved one to come out of darkness and into the light of the glorious gospel of Christ. I pray that the light of the gospel would shine on them and they would be turned from darkness to light and turned from the power of satan to God. I pray that they might receive forgiveness for their sins and an inheritance among those who are being sanctified by faith (Acts 26:18).

I command every veil and every form of spiritual blindness to be removed from their eyes, and I pray that all my family members would come to their senses and escape snares of the enemy (2 Tim. 2:26). I believe that the scales are falling off their eyes right now in Jesus' name (Acts 9:18). I believe and confess that my husband and children will come to Christ and continue to live in Christ, being rooted and built up in Him and strengthened in the faith (Col. 2:6-7). My family members will become rooted and established in the love of Christ, and they will come to know with all the saints what are the width and length and depth and height of that love. They will know the love that surpasses all understanding and knowledge, and they will be filled with all the fullness of God (Eph. 3:18-19).

I believe that my household will love the Lord with all their heart, with all their soul, with all their strength and with all their mind (Luke 10:27). My family will love others and love one another, just as You have loved us, and we will never pay back a wrong for a wrong, but we will be kind to each other and to everyone else (1 Thes. 5:15). I thank You, Father, that according to Ephesians 2:10, we are Your workmanship, created in Christ Jesus for good works, which God prepared beforehand that we should walk in them. Help us to walk in every good work You have foreordained for us to walk in. Prepare the way in front of us and remove every stumbling block and obstacle, in the name of Jesus.

Lord, in Psalms 112:2-3, You have said that the descendants of the man or woman that fears the Lord will be mighty on the earth. Cause my children to rise up and do mighty works for Your name. Cause them to become imitators of God and to walk in love (Eph. 5:1-2). Cause my children to flee youthful lusts and pursue righteousness, faith, love and peace with those who call on the Lord out of a pure heart (2 Tim. 2:22). Cause all my children to deny ungodliness and worldly lusts, and to live soberly, righteously and godly in the present age (Tit. 2:11-12). Cause everyone in my family to give attention to Your words and incline their ears to Your sayings (Prov. 4:20). When my children turn to the right or to the left, cause them to hear a voice behind them saying, "This is the way; walk in it" (Is. 30:21).

Furthermore, Lord, cause all of us to be filled with all joy and peace because we trust in You, and may we overflow with hope by the power of the Holy Spirit (Rom. 15:13). May we continually offer sacrifices of praise to You, and may the fruit of our lips confess Your Name. May we never forget to do good and to share with others (Heb. 13:15-16).

Father, I believe that my children and my household are blessed with every spiritual blessing in the heavenly places in Christ. I believe my children were chosen in Christ from the foundation of the world, that they should be holy and without blame before Him in love. For they have been predestined to be adopted by God as sons and daughters according to the pleasure of God's will (Eph. 1:3-5). And I believe that all my sons and daughters will willingly choose to walk into that destiny in the name of Jesus.

I pray that whatever my children find to do, they would work at it with all their hearts, as working for the Lord and not for men (Col. 3:23). Furthermore, I believe that Your divine power has given us all things pertaining to life and godliness, and that through the knowledge of You, we have been called to glory and to virtue (2 Pet. 1:3).

Heavenly Father, please help us to live in that glory and according to Your standard of virtue. Show us Your ways and teach us Your paths; lead us in Your truth and teach us. For You are the God of my salvation, and on You, I wait all the day (Ps. 25:4-5). I will trust in the LORD with all my heart. I will lean not to my own understanding, but in all my ways I will acknowledge You, and I believe You will direct my paths and the paths of my children (Prov. 3:5-6). I believe the steps of the godly are directed by the Lord, and You delight in every detail of our lives (Ps. 37:23).

I believe, that just like Jesus, my children shall daily be increasing in wisdom, in stature, and in favor with God and man (Luke 2:52). I declare that my children shall be true worshippers of the Lord, and they will worship the Father in spirit and in truth (John 4:23). I believe the work of righteousness will be peace, and the effect of righteousness, quietness and assurance forever. My household will dwell in a peaceful habitation, in a secure dwelling and in quiet resting places with God (Is. 32:17-18). I confess and believe that You will go before us and make the crooked places straight; You will break in pieces the gates of bronze and cut the bars of iron (Is. 45:2). In other words, You will destroy every stronghold the enemy tries to erect in our lives.

I declare by faith, according to Jeremiah 31:17, that there is hope in my future and hope for my family and my children. All my children shall come back to God and back to their spiritual borders. All my children shall be taught by the LORD, and great shall be the peace and undisturbed composure of my children (Is. 54:13). For I am persuaded that You are well able to keep all that I have committed to You in prayer (2 Tim. 1:12). I commit my family to You, God, and I trust You will perform these things that I am praying. I pray that You would make the righteousness of those in my household to shine like the dawn, and the justice of our cause like the noonday sun (Ps. 37:5-6).

Furthermore, Father, I pray that my children would listen to counsel and receive instruction, that they would be wise all the days of their lives (Prov. 19:20). I pray that the Lord's counsel would stand in their lives (Prov. 19:21). Lord, You said in Proverbs 22:6, "Train up a child in the way he should go, and when he is old he will not depart from it." Therefore, I believe that You will bring my children in remembrance of the truths they were taught in their youth, and You will convict them of truth in their inner man. I believe that You will teach us, O Lord, to follow Your decrees and to keep them to the end. You will give us understanding, and we will keep Your law and obey it with all our hearts. Direct us in the path of Your commandments. Turn our hearts toward Your statutes and not toward selfish gain. Turn our eyes away from worthless things and preserve our lives according to Your Word (Ps. 119:33-37). Help us to do nothing out of selfish ambition or vain conceit but in humility to consider others better than ourselves (Philippians 2:3).

Father, I also pray that you would set a guard over the mouth of every person in my home (Ps. 141:3). I pray that everyone in my family would not allow any unwholesome talk to come out of their mouths, but only what is helpful for building others up (Eph. 4:29). May the words of our mouths and the meditation of our hearts be pleasing in Your sight, O Lord, my Rock and my Redeemer (Ps. 19:14). Cause us to always speak the truth in love, so that we may grow up in all things into Him who is the head—Christ (Eph. 4:15).

Furthermore, I pray that the God of our Lord Jesus Christ, the Father of glory, may give to everyone in my household, the spirit of wisdom and revelation in the knowledge of who You are, and that the eyes of our understanding would be enlightened and flooded with light. I pray that we would know what is the hope of our calling in Christ, and what are the riches of the glory of the inheritance that is ours in Christ Jesus (Eph. 1:17-18).

Cause my children to incline their ears, to hear the words of the wise and to apply their hearts to knowledge (Prov. 22:17). For, like the Apostle John, I have no greater joy than to hear that my children walk in truth (3 John 4). And if my children are lacking wisdom in any area, cause them to ask God, who gives to all liberally and without reproach, and it will be given to them (James 1:5). I pray that the Spirit of the LORD would rest upon my husband and children. I pray they would possess the Spirit of wisdom and understanding, the Spirit of counsel and might, the Spirit of knowledge and of the fear of the LORD (Is. 11:2). I pray for this seven-fold Spirit of God to fall upon my whole household in power. I invite the Holy Spirit to fill my home at all times and continually teach us and train us about the way we should be living before the Lord.

I pray for the blessing, the anointing and favor of God to come upon my household. I believe that I am blessed with believing Abraham according to Galatians 3:9, and because I am blessed, I believe my household is also blessed. I speak the blessing of God over my home and family: blessed shall be my family. We will not walk in the counsel of the ungodly, nor shall we stand in the path of sinners. We will not sit in the seat of the scornful. Instead, our delight shall be in the law of the LORD, and in His law we will meditate day and night. Therefore, everyone in my household shall be like a tree planted by the rivers of water. They will bring forth fruit in its season. Their leaves shall not wither, and whatever they do shall prosper (Ps. 1:1-3).

I confess and believe that my children shall be the head and not the tail. They will live above only and not beneath. I pray that they would always heed the commandments of the LORD and would be careful to observe them (Deut. 28:13). Cause my children to be blessed in the city, blessed in the country, blessed in the fruit of their body and the produce of their ground. Increase all that they set their hands to do and bless their food supplies. Cause them to be blessed when they come in and blessed when they go out (Deut. 28:3-6).

Father, in the name of Jesus, I acknowledge that You have set before us life and death, blessing and cursing; therefore, I pray that everyone in my household would choose life and that they would love the LORD. I pray that we would obey Your voice, and cling to You, for You are our life and the length of our days (Deut. 30:19-20). Furthermore, I believe that You God will cause all things to work together for good for me and for my household because we love the Lord and are called according to Your purpose (Rom. 8:28). I believe that You will go before us and be with us; You will never leave us nor forsake us (Deut. 31:8). And I pray that You would never allow mercy and truth to forsake us. Instead, help us to bind Your promises around our necks and write them on the tablet of our hearts (Prov. 3:3). With this, I conclude this prayer, and I believe that You cause Your Word to accomplish and prosper in the thing for which it is sent (Is. 55:11). In the name of Jesus, Amen!!

About Dr. Christi Butler

Dr. Butler has been serving the Lord in Christian ministry since 1997. For many years, Christi conducted evangelistic outreaches and church services within several California State prisons. Over the years, Christi has founded three non-profit corporations and has been active as a church leader, pastor, teacher and evangelist. Christi is currently ordained through Kingsway Fellowship International (KFI). She holds a B.A. and M.A. degree in Theology, as well as a Doctorate of Ministry degree from Vision International College and Seminary. Christi has a secondary Bachelor of Science in Management degree from the University of Phoenix. Dr. Butler is passionate about sharing her faith and seeing the Lord Jesus Christ glorified through all her ministry endeavors. Chrisi lives with her family in Murrieta, California.

Praying on the Armor of God for You and Your Spouse!

By Dorothy Fleming

I often "pray on" the Armor of God (Ephesians 6) not just for me but for my husband as well. It is very powerful to pray God's Word back to Him, and He reminds us that His word will not return to Him void but will accomplish what He desires in us (Isaiah 55:11) and in our spouses! This is an awesome weapon against the evil one. We cover not only ourselves with God's Armor, but provide protection for our spouses! How I pray on my armor changes as well as the verses I'm led to pray, depending upon what life circumstances I'm facing. Join me and let's pray on the armor daily with the Lord's power, love and protection for ourselves and our spouses!

Belt of Truth: Dear Lord, please help me to remember this day that Your Son Jesus is beside me, and You will uphold me with Your righteous right hand (Isaiah 41:10). You go before me and follow me (Psalm 139:5). You will show me the path where I should walk this day. You will point out the right road for me to follow. You will lead me by your truth and teach me, for You are the God who saves me. All day long my hope is in You (Psalm 25:4-5), as I trust in You for (spouse's) salvation.

Breastplate of Righteousness: I put on the Breastplate of Righteousness to protect my heart, which belongs to Jesus. Please help me to guard my heart above all else, for I know that everything I do flows from it (Proverbs 4:23) and that my mouth will speak what fills my heart. Please help me to be a reflection of the love of Your Son Jesus to (spouse) this day, Oh Lord!

Helmet of Salvation: I pray that the Helmet of Salvation will protect my mind and my thoughts this day. That the words of my mouth and the meditation of my heart be pleasing in Your sight, O Lord, my Rock and my Redeemer (Psalm 19:14). Please help me to remember that

You will keep in perfect peace those whose minds are steadfast because they trust in You (Isaiah 26:3). Please help me to trust in You, O Lord, for (spouse's) salvation.

Feet Fitted with the Gospel of Peace: That I may know and proclaim Your Word to those You place in my path, O Lord, especially (spouse). I pray that the Holy Spirit will be with me and that You will grant me the wisdom to recognize the opportunities placed before me this day and the courage to be obedient to Your commands. Please help me to be the aroma of Christ (2 Corinthians 2:15) to (spouse) and help me to remember that You love (spouse) more than I do. You do not want anyone to perish, for You want everyone, including (spouse), to be saved (2 Peter 3:9). I pray that You will put people of peace in (spouse's) path today.

Shield of Faith: Please help me, Lord, to use my Shield of Faith to extinguish the flaming arrows that the devil hurls at me and (spouse). Please help me to remember that the devil has no power over me, and that You have not given me a spirit of fear and timidity but of power, love and self-discipline (2 Timothy 1:7)! I pray Your protection on us both, O Lord. Please command Your guardian angels to walk with each of us this day (Psalm 91:11).

Sword of the Word: For me, Lord, Your word is my most powerful weapon against the devil's attempts to steal, kill and destroy (John 10:10). But he has no power over me because I have been redeemed by the blood of Your Son, Christ Jesus. I pray that the Holy Spirit will continue to work in me, creating an ever-burning desire to know Your word and commit it my heart that it may be ever on my lips (Psalm 34:1). Please keep me from becoming weary of doing good, for at the proper time I will reap a harvest if I do not give up (Galatians 6:9)! Please help me, O Lord, to never give up!!! Lord, I ask that You will give (spouse) a heart to know You, and You will be (spouse's) God, and he will return to You with all his heart (Jeremiah 24:7).

About Dorothy Fleming

I live in Texas with Alan, my loving husband of 27 years! We have a furry, four-legged rescued family. I take our 80-pound dog, Teddy along with our blind cat, Iris, to visit our local nursing home several times a month. I love outdoor activities and also yoga. I love to cross-stitch or crochet while watching old movies with my husband. I have grown in my faith through participating in small church groups and studying God's Word. In 2012, after reading quite a few books on unequally yoked marriage, I found *Winning Him Without Words* and have been thankful to call Lynn and Dineen friends ever since!

Part IV:
Victory Prayer Strategies

By Faith and Not Sight

By Ramona Fredericks

Lord, I pray for Godly wisdom for my husband.

Thank you, Lord, for giving him wisdom and knowledge, not as the world gives it, but as You give it, so he would understand Your children.

Thank You, Lord, for making Him a servant of God, for by serving You, he would know how to serve his family—at home, at church, and at work.

Thank You, Lord, for making him a lover of Your Word, for loving Your Word is loving You, for You are Your Word. Your Word gives insight, understanding, and strength, and it renews minds to bring good change.

Thank You, Lord, for blessing my husband with a relationship with the Holy Spirit so he may walk in obedience and instruction and in Your will.

Thank You for making him a man of integrity, so that Your Spirit is seen in him all the days of his life. Thank You for making him a good husband, who is faithful, loves His wife more than himself, kind, understanding and teaches his wife in the ways of God.

Thank You for making him a good father. Who knows better than You how to be a good father? Teach him how to listen, instruct and love his children in Your ways. Be an example of obedience and joy to him.

Thank You for making Him a good son to You, so He may be a son who loves and spends time with his own mother.

Thank You for making him a good brother, so he may be a good example to his siblings, brothers, and sisters in the kingdom.

Thank You, Lord, for making him a good friend, so he may be a friend who is not afraid to teach and keep his friends accountable in the ways of God.

Thank You for making him a good employee, free from an Egyptian spirit and mindset, and filled with the desire to accomplish things with joy and to be pleasing unto You.

Thank You most of all, Lord, for making him Yours—a man of love, truth and a man who hungers for God.

Thank You, Daddy Jesus, for hearing Your daughter's prayer and answering it in Your way and not mine, in Your time and not mine. May I praise You and trust You while You work. Amen!

About Ramona Fredericks

I am Ramona Fredericks. My husband Grant and I will be married for 14 years in September 2016. I have three children, two boys (13 and 11) and the youngest, a little girl of eight. I wrote this prayer after my husband cheated on me, 14 days before our divorce was finalized. I instituted the divorce, however, he did not want a divorce. I told God, "I could not go on with the same man, as I saw no love in him for me."

Then the Holy Spirit told me to pray, as I would like him to be. Therefore, I prayed this prayer. By God's grace, we are still married, and still have a lot of work ahead. So I keep adding to this prayer. God is faithful to change what I cannot in me and my husband. Ramona lives with her family in South Africa.

On These Promises

By Dee Rusnak

Hope. That's what seems to dissolve so quickly as I wait month after weary month, year after year, for my husband's salvation. I needed hope. A hope that would endure.

I found myself in a dark, dry and desolate place. I felt utterly alone. And I felt as though I was the only one walking this painful path. I wanted off! I wanted to be like everyone else—serving God alongside my husband, knee-deep in ministry. In my mind, I could not serve God any other way and failed to see my own home as a mission field, ripe for the harvest.

My focus was on me. . .poor, lonely me.

One day, out of the blue, the Lord led me to the SUM website, where hope was plentiful! There were many others just like me! They were on the same path, telling my stories! Their hearts yearned with the same desperate voice as mine. Their eyes were on the Lord Jesus, not their husbands or themselves. They were standing on God's promises from His Word. Daily they encouraged with scripture after scripture, revealing God's love for the unsaved and His plan for their salvation.

Hope came alive!

The Lord led me to a verse I had written down many years ago: *"Call to Me, and I will answer you, and show you great and mighty things, which you do not know (Jeremiah 33:3)."* He took me further into Jeremiah 33 to verse six, *"I will bring health and healing; I will heal them and reveal to them the abundance of peace and truth."* Then to verse eight, *"I will cleanse them from all their iniquity by which they have sinned against Me, and I will pardon all their iniquities by which they have sinned and by which they have transgressed against Me."* And further on to verses 10-11, *"Again there shall be heard in this place – of which you say, 'It is desolate'.. .the voice of joy and the voice of gladness, the voice of the bridegroom and the voice of the bride, the voice of those who will say: 'Praise the Lord of hosts, for the Lord is good, for His mercy endures forever.'"* (NKJV)

On these promises, I pray: Dear Heavenly Father, You beckon me to call upon You, to come to You, to seek You, to cry out to You, to rest in You and You hear me. You incline Your ear and listen to my troubled heart, collecting my tears, knowing my deepest desires and desperation, holding me close.

While I await the salvation of my husband, I sometimes lose hope. A failed hope that focuses on everything but You, as I surround myself with my own loneliness. You alone give me hope. You alone ARE my hope. For reasons only You know, You have chosen me first. You have caused me to see with my heart . . . to see YOU and Your perspective! YOU are with me! I am not alone, nor will I ever be! This is the path chosen for me, and we will walk joyfully together, knowing You are at work continuously.

My service to the Kingdom is not in the things I can do but in accepting and embracing what You created especially for me. You have shown me that many great and mighty things, which were inaccessible before, will be revealed to my husband. Only You, who are spiritual, can reveal these things to him, giving understanding, enlightening the mind, granting repentance and warming the heart. In Your great mercy, You reach down to the lost while they stumble in their world of darkness, delivering them from an enemy not seen and setting their feet firmly upon a rock. Just as You did for me.

Nothing is too hard for You, Lord. I pray for my husband to be open to receive all You have for him. He has no idea just how lost he really is as he seeks to find comfort and safety in the deceitful prison where so many are dwelling.

Awaken him, Lord, to Your truths!

Cause him to be desperate for a Savior. Convict his heart, not to shame, but to be cleansed and healed. Bring him, Lord, into Your loving family of believers. I pray this in Your precious name. Amen!

About Dee Rusnak

My name is Dee Rusnak. My husband and I have been married 44 years and live in Westerville, Ohio. We have three handsome sons and three adorable grandchildren—with another one on the way! I've been waiting and praying 22 years for my husband's salvation. My hope is in my God, who can do all things!

Sprinkle Clean Water Upon My Wife

Jan 20/17

By Ian Acheson

"I will sprinkle clean water on you, and you will be clean; I will cleanse you from all your impurities and from all your idols.
I will give you a new heart and put a new spirit in you; I will remove from you a heart of stone and give you a heart of flesh.
And I will put My Spirit in you and move you to follow My decrees and be careful to keep My laws. Then you will live in the land I gave your ancestors; you will be My people, and I will be your God. I will save you from all your uncleanness. I will call for the grain and make it plentiful and will not bring famine

upon you. I will increase the fruit of the trees and the crops of the field so that you will no longer suffer disgrace among the nations because of famine." — *Ezekiel 36:25-30*

Jesus, we love You, we worship You. We praise You for Your fierce love for us and our spouses. Your intense love surrounds us all, all of the time, 24 by 7. You can't stop loving us. And You desire to dwell in our hearts. You are sprinkling us clean, making us holy, transforming us and renewing us.

Thank you!

Thank you!

Thank you!

We bring our spouses before You. They don't know You yet. They don't know how much You love them. They don't need religion. They need the gospel, and they need to know how much You love them and how much they need You. Please reveal to them Your love and their need for You.

Sprinkle clean water on them so they will be clean. Please cleanse them from all impurities and from all their idols. Forgive them their sins, dear Lord.

You are the Author and Perfecter of our faith. Be the Author and Perfecter of their faith. Replace their hearts of stone with hearts of flesh by giving them a new spirit. Your Spirit. The Holy Spirit. Holy Comforter and Counselor.

Holy Spirit, our spouses can only come to know the gospel of grace by Your handy work. Impart the revelation of Your grace in their hearts. Tear the veil that shrouds their hearts from top to bottom and shatter the scales that cover their eyes. Humble them with Your grace. Reveal your bountiful beauty. Stun them with Your extravagant love for them.

Father, increase the fruit and crops of their fields, as You free them to fulfill Your purpose. May Your kingdom come; Your will be done in their lives as it is in heaven. To Your glory. And only to Your glory.

In the precious, loving name of Jesus. Amen!

About Ian Acheson

Ian resides in Sydney, Australia, and shares life with his wife, Fiona. They have two grown sons and one delightful daughter-in-law. They keep busy with their two dogs, both cross-kelpies. Ian is the author of, *Angelguard*, the first installment in the *Chronicles of the Angelguard* series. In addition, Ian writes regularly for a variety of writer's blogs, plus at SpirituallyUnequalMarriage.com. When not writing, Ian is a strategy consultant.

Part V:
Prayer Strategies For the Spiritually Mismatched Heart

Have You Forgotten Me Lord?

By Martha Bush

My heart was so burdened for my husband's salvation, and I felt the urgency to fast and pray.
The fast turned into weeks and then into months.

Hunger pains were overtaking me, but there was no manifestation of peace over his salvation.
"Where are you?" I cried. "Have You forgotten me, Lord?"

God replied through a prophetic word that was spoken to me.
"No more fasting, weeping, sackcloth and ashes.
Just as Jehoshaphat went into the battle, did I not send ambush and did not the enemy kill itself? (2 Chronicles 20)
So, pick yourself up and rejoice in the Lord. It is a day of victory, a day of praise."

But, Lord, as I have prayed many times,
that prophetic word and the promise was given to me on February 3, 1988.
As of this date, that was 28 years ago.
"Have You forgotten me, Lord?"

Even with the promise, the trials continued to come.
To be honest, Lord, the trials became worse after Your promise was made.
Deep down inside, I know it is the enemy trying to make me give up.
While at the same time, I cry out, "Have You forgotten me, Lord?"

The years have gone by; our girls are grown and serving You.
My heart broke when Hannah was four and asked, "Nana, how come Granddaddy doesn't go to church? He is not going to know Jesus!"
You know, it would be so nice to have him sitting beside our family in the pews.
Why is it taking so long? "Have You forgotten me, Lord?"

Now it's not about whether he will be saved; You promised me he would.
I just hate to see all those gifts You have given him going to waste.
It is also about the three of us enjoying life together—me, You and him.
You know, we are not getting any younger; "Have You forgotten me, Lord?"

Okay, Lord, I'm through with all my complaints for today; time to get back into Your presence.
It's in Your presence that I have heard You speak many times.
"Be patient a little longer, My child; just like I did for Abraham, I'm going to give you an Isaac.
Through your husband's story, many will be saved, and My name will be glorified."

"No, I have not forgotten you."

The Story Behind the Prayer

It was 1987, and Evangelist Mickie Bonner came to Community Church in Orange, Texas, where my teenage girls and I attended. He conducted a study on "Spiritual Warfare." During one of his sermons, he suddenly asked a question that grabbed my attention regarding my unsaved husband. "Women, how would you like your husband saved? Keep your mouth shut to him, pray only to the Lord."

He continued by saying, "You should fast and pray until that prayer is manifested, or until you receive a release in your spirit that God has heard you."

And so it was, in the coming days, I was overcome with an overwhelming urgency that I'd better fast and pray for my husband's salvation now!

This intensity and urgency went on for about three months. After three months, I finally prayed one night: "Lord, I am so tired and hungry, but he is not saved yet, and I don't feel any peace about his ever being saved. What am I to do?"

I began to listen to a tape by Sylvia Thompson, a minister, whose Bible studies I attended weekly. The series of tapes was entitled "How to Pray." She stated that there are many ways to pray, but ended by saying that the best prayer she had ever experienced was in the passage of scripture found in 2 Chronicles 20:1-22.

Briefly summarized:

- (vs 1) An army was coming against Jehoshaphat and Israelites.
- (vs 3) Jehoshaphat feared and set himself to seek the Lord and proclaimed a fast.
- (vs 14) Jehaziel spoke: Be not afraid, the battle is not yours, but God's.
- (vs 17) No need to fight. Stand still and see the salvation of the Lord.
- (vs 22) The Israelites went into battle singing praises, and the enemy was killed.

As I pondered this Old Testament passage, I noted that I had almost completed the list in this passage the last three months of my life.

1. I had feared the Lord (referenced), recognizing Him and my need of His help against this army coming against my husband.
2. I had fasted.
3. My question now was: "Is it time to praise?"

I went to my weekly Bible study with Sylvia the following morning. Right in the middle of praise and worship, a prophetic word came forth to me, verbatim from the passage of scripture in 2 Chronicles 20. I immediately received it as a release in my spirit and went out to the finest restaurant in town and had a scrumptious meal to celebrate.

My prayer actually summarizes the talks I have had with God over the years concerning this scripture and prophetic word.

About Martha Bush

I live in Orange, Texas, where I lead a SUM Group. My husband and I have been married 50 years, are the parents of two daughters and are now grandparents of four. Last, but not least, we are privileged to have two wonderful Christian sons-in-law.

I See the Walls Breaking Down

By Maira Zantidis

Jesus, since the day we first met and all the days after leading to this great love affair, You placed the desire in my heart to seek a man who seeks Your heart. What I thought I wanted then was too limited for the limitless Provider that You are. My plan was too small for the greater plan You prepared for me. I praise You for every heartache in my past, because through them, You equipped me to take care of the man You brought into my life.

The more I know You, the more I understand Your desire to nurture those who are lost. A lost soul to You is what a stolen child is to its mother. You could have led me to someone who already knew You (that would have been easier). Instead, You entrusted me with Your 'stolen child.' You provided me with all the resources to help lead my husband back to You through the life of Jesus. Lord, You gave me a purpose. Knowing that You brought me to this place with this man at my side, I am comforted that he is on his way to knowing You. And You are also changing him from someone who didn't know a relationship with You was possible, into a man who seeks Your heart. Lord, he may not know it now, but I see more of You in him every day. I see the walls breaking down and his heart opening up. Truly, no darkness can stand Your light, Father. Allow it to shine over every inch of us, our home and our family.

In the beginning I was an infant, stumbling as I asked You again and again for a Christian man. You told me, "Wait." I didn't realize it until now, but the longer You made me wait, the bigger and better Your plan became. Lord, I couldn't see before that You were preparing him for Your little girl, because You love me so much. As I grew, the time came that I began to walk. In that moment, I stopped praying for myself and began to pray for those You placed upon my heart. My cries to You are no longer selfish. You removed selfishness from me, because the man You gave me does not deserve a selfish wife. You want me to be compassionate, forgiving, enduring and patient, so You can show the man I have come to love who You are through me. Give me the continuing desire to serve others and be the example You want me to be for my husband's sake. Only with Your hand on my heart and Your Spirit guiding me will I be deserving of the gift of my husband. I am overwhelmed that You have honored me with the responsibility to safely guide my husband toward You with love and prayer. You chose me and thought me strong enough to endure all the tough times that would surely come our way. I can't praise you enough. Hallelujah!

Father, You taught me who I am in You. You gave me purpose in life, because, for me, there is no death. I am covered in the blood of Christ that unites me with You for all eternity. No weapon formed against me will prosper. There is no room for doubt in our home or our hearts. Continue to renew my heart, Lord, and penetrate the walls that surround my spouse. Leave no room for the enemy to enter our home to destroy the miraculous changes I see in him day-after-day. Push me further, Lord, with the desire to intercede for others. Equip me to be a warrior who is unafraid to stand up to our enemy with the authority given to me by Jesus Christ—the Author of my Salvation. I now run this race with renewed purpose. I break the bonds that separate my husband from grace, because we have been saved once and for all, purified and made holy.

My Father, my Shepherd, You picked me up when I felt worthless. You breathed life into me again. You washed me in water. You put me through the fire and made me clean, shiny and perfect, as You always intended.

As I call out to You, whether things are easy or difficult, I lift my husband up to You. Always remembering that he is not mine to keep but Yours for me to help nurture. This is why I praise YOU with authentic joy because even when I feel I am alone, I am not! Your name is Yahweh. Your name is eternal, unchangeable and covenant-keeping. You made a covenant of salvation through the blood of Christ, just as You made a covenant to unite my husband and me to make us one. United as one, the blood of Your salvation that covers me also covers my husband.

About Maira Zantidis

Many years before my husband and I met, he was in a coma from a car accident, his girlfriend died, and he suffered from selective amnesia. Everyone told him he should have died. He himself believed he died and came back to life. For 15 years my husband searched for answers. He knew he had been given a second chance but had no idea why or what to do with this miracle.

One day he asked me why I care for him as I do, and without hesitation, I answered, "Jesus gave you a second chance. If He has entrusted someone so important to me, then I don't want to mess it up. I have to take care of my Father's gifts."

I witnessed a change in my husband after hearing those words—words he'd never heard before—which also impacted me. It was a revelation to both of us!

Maira lives with her husband in Illinois.

The Table

By Barb Twigg

Recently we bought a new mattress. I set the date for delivery and planned on removing the dust ruffle to have it washed and ready to put under the new mattress when it arrived.

I remembered a long while ago I had read somewhere, perhaps at the SUM website, to write out your heartfelt prayer for your husband and place it under the mattress so that he is soaked in the power of prayer—something along those lines. So, I wanted to make sure to get that prayer out from under the mattress. I retrieved it, placed it in my bible and then the next morning, I read through it again. I thought, "Wow, that is a really beautiful and heartfelt prayer. It covers all the bases of prayer for my husband."

This prayer was filled with Scripture, love, tears and truth, as well as fight and faith beyond what I feel today! As I reread my prayer (originally written in 2014), it kind of made me sad. Where was I now? I guess since I've been with this same man for 31 years and have been unequally yoked our entire marriage, I experience seasons of weariness. The devil started picking at my mind and slowly, over these past two years, my passion for my husband's salvation has turned lukewarm.

Some days I'm on fire and mad that satan has blinded him, and I victoriously yell at satan, "NO YOU CAN'T HAVE HIM!" I guess I feel as though I don't know how to pray for him differently to see results. And therein lies the whole truth. The whole problem. The results are not up to me.

I had a dream that I was in a "party" atmosphere, and my husband was close by me. A lady was praying and looking toward heaven. My husband looked perplexed. He left my side and she turned to me and asked, "What is your prayer of faith?"

I immediately replied, "To see my husband saved."

She then said something like, "Your answer is too scripted." I then awoke with a yearning for her to tell me how to pray differently.

As I contemplated my dream, the Lord gave me a new prayer.

You, God, love my husband with an everlasting love. You, Lord, invite my husband to your table. This table offers forgiveness and mercy and no condemnation. This table has been set for him so that he will know he is loved by the one, true God! This table is set for my spouse that he may see how pleased his Heavenly Father is of him. This table has been set for him to be praised and accepted.

Oh God, his earthly father was a terrible example to my husband. But, God, You are the only one who matters. This table that You have laid out for my man comes with LOVE. Everlasting, soaking, penetrating, oozing acceptance and love like no earthly father can ever provide.

You say: come and eat, feast on the bread of life that no human can give. You say: I am good, I am all you need. You can trust Me, the I AM.

I AM is My name in all the earth. I AM can redeem, restore and heal. I AM your new way of thinking. I AM the voice you are hearing in your heart. I AM calling for You, son of mine, come and let Me lavish you with all that you have been set apart to receive. No longer deny My love for you. No longer deny your trust in ME.

Have Your way, Father. I trust You with my husband. I know what I know, my faith is big and You are bigger! Amen!

About Barb Twigg

Lover of Christ since. . .a long time! Back slid and rededicated 15 years ago! We have been married for 31 years with no children. We live in Texas and are truly blessed.

Staying Connected to Your Spouse
By Dineen Miller

So again I say, each man must love his wife as he loves himself,
and the wife must respect her husband. — Ephesians 5:33
(For complete reference, read Ephesians 5:21-33)

You're two people sitting in a restaurant, enjoying a night out, spending time together. No time wasted preparing food—just the menu to read. No kids to interfere—just the occasional bad timing of the waiter. And no responsibility other than to sit and enjoy each other's company—just the two of you.

But then you suddenly realize you have nothing to share. Every bit of your world is permeated by the presence of God. And your spouse, well, not so much. What do you say? How do you connect? What do you do?

I remember this moment. And to be honest, it scared me. My husband and I had always been communicators. Great communicators actually. Over the years, friends and family commented on this aspect of our relationship often. We always shared a lot and had a lot to talk about.

But as my faith grew deeper, my focus and interests changed significantly. I could spend hours talking to another believer about God and His love and goodness. Testimonies are fun and inspiring! But when your spouse doesn't share your belief in Jesus or isn't really interested in pursuing a deeper faith life, a gap can form—a disconnect.

The first step to reestablish an intimate connection with our spouse is not to ignore it. Acknowledge the disconnect and talk to God about it. One of the best pieces of advice the Holy Spirit inspired me with was don't identify my spiritually mismatched marriage by the spiritual mismatch. If that's the only way we see and identify our marriage, then we miss the blessings God is pouring into a marriage He intends to thrive and grow beyond this limitation. Don't limit God.

As much as we want to connect to our spouse spiritually, they're not able to—yet. So look for other ways to reconnect and spend time together. Take walks, play games, look for ways to share your world in a way with your spouse that he or she can relate to and look for ways to enter their world and show interest in what he or she likes.

Father God, thank You for my spouse. I love him/her and want our marriage to be a rich place of love, compassion and safety. Lord, we are one in Your sight (Eph 5:31). Pour Your great love through me so that my spouse can experience Your amazing love first hand.

Wife's Prayer: I pray that You would help my husband to love me as You love the church, Lord Jesus (Eph 5:25).

Husband's Prayer: Help me be a man worthy of my wife's respect and help her to trust and respect me as I grow more and more Christ-like (Eph 5:22-24).

Holy Spirit, inspire unity between us. Inspire us with unique and fun ideas of how to stay connected and to share our lives well. Be present and fill us with Your fruit of love, joy, peace, patience, kindness, gentleness and self-control (Gal 5:22). Make our marriage a place of romance and deep friendship. In the name of Jesus, amen!

About Dineen Miller

Dineen is passionate about God's Word and truth. She's been featured on the Moody Radio Network, Focus on the Family Radio, Dr. James Dobson's FamilyTalk, FamilyLife Today and INSIGHT on Miracle Channel. She is the coauthor of the award-winning book, *Winning Him Without Words* and *Not Alone: Trusting God to Raise Godly Kids in a Spiritually Mismatched Home*. She is also the author of the ACFW Carol Award winning book, *The Soul Saver*. She and her husband love to collect shells and walk the famous white sands of Siesta Key Beach, Florida. Visit Dineen online at SpirituallyUnequalMarriage.com and DineenMiller.com.

Bless My Husband

by Heather Passuello

Heavenly Father,

Thank You so much for the blessing that my husband is to me. I am truly grateful for the wonderful father he is becoming to our child. Especially, when I consider that he didn't have the greatest examples in his own life.

Lord, I pray for wisdom for my husband to be the father that You've called him to be. I ask that he and I come together in our decisions when it comes to parenting and that we honor You in those decisions. Thank You for Your patience with us when we mess up. Please help us to forgive ourselves and each other in those moments.

Lord, I pray that as we travel this journey of "parenthood" that we will not lose sight of the blessing You gave us in our precious child(ren). Guide us as we set an example for them and help us to honor You through all of it, even when we aren't aware. Let Your powerful presence be in our home and our work, and everywhere we go. Let Your presence be evident to all. Your Word says that my spouse and children are sanctified through just one believer. I am grateful for that promise and the hope it provides me. I pray that both my husband and daughter would come to love You as time passes and to ask You to live in their hearts. As 2 Peter 3:9 says, You are not slow in keeping Your promises and You are patient with each of us, wanting all to repent, I am very grateful for that reminder.

I am not always faithful in praying for my spouse and child(ren), but You are always faithful in everything. Lord, I ask that my husband allows forgiveness to penetrate his heart and replace bitterness. I also declare that any generational curses in his family and my own be broken and thrown into the eternal hellfire and to never return, in Jesus' name. I pray that we look to Your example of love and parenting as we often struggle through this life.

Father God, please protect my husband in the workplace. Not only physically but spiritually and emotionally as well. Set a guard over his lips to speak honoring, kind and loving words to all he encounters. Help him to resist any temptations he may encounter. Please help him make honorable decisions, even if it costs him a great deal. Honoring You is more important than anything. I know that You will provide all our needs, and I ask that You would speak this truth into my husband's heart.

God, You are so good. So loving. So kind. Help us all to be more like You. You have blessed our family a great deal, and I ask that You help us to be a blessing to all we encounter. Help us to be less of ourselves and more of You. Thank You for Your provision, love and abundant mercy over all of us. I will praise You all of my days, and my hope is in You that You will woo my husband and child(ren) so they choose to live a life for You. I humbly pray all of this in Jesus' name. Amen!

About Heather Passuello

My name is Heather Passuello. I live in rural Pennsylvania and I am the Administrative Assistant at my church, Harvest Family Fellowship. I am married to my high school sweetheart who is a wonderful husband and father. I currently have one child, Joanna, but I am praying for more. My husband believes in God but has yet to accept Christ into his heart and start a relationship with Jesus. I have been involved in women's ministry for two years and have also been a part of the worship team at my church. Currently, I am discovering more of who I am as God created me and learning to embrace that part of who I am.

Prepare the Soil and Send the Rain

By Gillian Russell Meisner

This prayer is a combination of many different prayers I've prayed for my husband over the years.

One morning the Holy Spirit took over my prayers and I prayed something different, "Lord, prepare his heart for the good gifts You want to give him—passion, wisdom and a holy fear of You so powerful, it completely changes the direction of his life. Amen!"

Soon after, I awoke in the middle of the night with these four words: *Hope, I've added water.* The Holy Spirit led me to the passage of the woman at the well, and the Lord spoke to my heart, "The water which I will give him will become in him a spring of water, welling up to eternal life."

Several years ago while driving home, the Lord spoke to me very clearly about my husband, "Only when you are willing to lay down your will, then your husband will know Me." Gulp! God built on this, showing me that I need to let my husband live freely, even to make mistakes if he is to be able to find God. I realized that I needed to let go in a deeper way. Then in the spring of 2016, God began speaking to me about my husband—deep spiritual things that I felt I had no right to know, but God wanted me to understand him better. God showed me that my husband's heart is closed to God. The Lord also showed me He can only touch my husband with His love and forgiveness *through* me. And that I am called to truly love him as Christ, freely, unconditionally and without limits.

Lord, thank You for bringing my husband and me together. Thank You for everything You're doing in his life. Thank You for loving me through him. Father, I am asking You to open my eyes to see my husband through Your eyes. Let me glimpse his brilliance, his heart, his goodness and his soul. Lord, let me view my husband through Your eyes of love today.

Lord, prepare the soil and continue to soften his heart. Holy Spirit, come upon him in a powerful way to fulfill every purpose God has for his life. Lord, I lift him before Your Throne of Grace, and with tears, I place myself at his side. In Your great mercy and in Your perfect planning and purposes, do whatever it takes to open his heart to faith and salvation, his knowledge and love of the Truth! May he know the truth and let the truth set him free! Birth in him the passion You long for him to have for You. Breathe into him, wisdom. Fill him to overflowing with the Holy Spirit, welling up to eternal life!

I pray that You would bless him abundantly and meet his needs today. Clear his mind and heart so he can hear from You today. Dispel the darkness that is all around, seeking to hush Your voice that is singing love over him. May the light of truth shine into his heart to replace the lies. Protect his heart from the negative influences that will be around him today and from the growing darkness in this world seeking to silence Your voice of love.

I pray that in time he would have a dynamic relationship with You, that he would be in agreement with Your holy will and with the Holy Spirit, and that he would love You with all his heart, mind, soul and strength. I pray this for myself and our children as well.

Lord, I know You have laid responsibilities on him, so I pray that You would continue to build him up and enable him to step up and face each one like a man and to fulfill them so that he would please You. I pray especially that he would be more present with us and that time with his family would become the most important thing to him, after You, of course! Lord, open his eyes to see these truths!

Lord Jesus, help my husband to love me as You call all husbands to love their wives, as Christ loved the church and gave Himself up for her. Help him to see that we are better together, working in unity under Christ, to care for each other and our children. And help me to love him as You love him, and more and more to lay down my life for him to know You, to give everything I have for this man, for his soul.

I pray that loving gestures and interactions between us—kind and gentle words, joy, peace, patience and understanding, friendship, deeper intimacy and honor—would become the norm in our marriage and in our home. Also, I ask for a spirit of prayer and spiritual intimacy in our marriage. Help us to live in unity and not division today. Lord, I pray for the peace of our home and the prosperity of our family. In the name of Jesus, amen!

About Gillian Russell Meisner

Gillian lives in Canada with her husband and four very lively little boys in training to be mighty warriors for God someday. She loves taking pictures, journaling, but is most passionate about her love for God and following His leading in her life. She tries to pour God's love into everything she does, and with Him, life is always an adventure!

Part VI:
Specific Strategic Prayers

Power Prayer Against Divorce
by Lynn Donovan

Many families have been ravaged by divorce. And the reality of this fact stirs up a Holy fire within my soul that I can only explain as the righteous anger of the Lord. The enemy has weaved his deceit upon God's people bringing his ministry to kill, steal and destroy, but NO MORE.

In my family, divorce has now reached into the fourth generation. My parents divorced, and my grandparents divorced in their 70's. I divorced when I was young and now my son is heading in that direction. I'm mad as you know what—and I'm not going to take it anymore!!!

Be warned devil. I'm taking away your authority to curse the generations of my family with the destruction of divorce. From this day forward, I revoke your authority to even breathe one word or deceive with lies, any of my family members to a thousand generations. Today, I draw a line in the sand and stand behind my Papa God and with His Son, my Savior Jesus, and by His name and power, I declare you have no authority to cause a divorce in my family line as of right now.

My friends, I'm convinced that we must take action and pray as the sanctified believer in our home. Today we take the authority given to us by Jesus and free our family from the work of the devil and demons, who are planting seeds of divorce.

Pray with me out loud:

In the name of the Lord Jesus Christ, I stand with Jesus at my side, and with angels prepared to move upon my spoken words of prayer and with the blessing and love of my Father God.

By the authority given to me in Luke 9:1-2, I declare the enemy, the devil and all demons, all their works and effects are hereby silenced. They have no authority now to lie to me or any of my family members about divorce. I cancel any and all agreements that believing their lies may have allowed influence in my life or the lives of my family.

Today, I declare the demonic must leave my home, my children and my marriage and go directly into the pit and be bound there forever.

I cancel all generational curses of my ancestors that may have allowed divorce to enter into my family line. I draw a line in the sand now and today. From this day forward our family line, the House of _____ (Donovan) is free from any evil influence, lies, or past agreements with the enemy about divorce. I slam shut any doors that were opened to let evil speak lies to me or have any bearing or influence upon me or my family.

In the name of the Lord Jesus Christ, I command all evil must depart from my home, my children and my husband and I command impure spirits to immediately go into the pit. In the name of the Lord Jesus Christ, there will be no replacement of evil in our lives now and forever.

And now, Lord, I fill those spaces where evil tried to harm with Your love. I release Your Holy Spirit now to come into the hearts of our home and fill every living area with Your presence. Open the portals of heaven and let the peace of Jesus pervade our hearts, souls and minds. Give us joy and flood every part of our home and being with Your love. Fill our home to be an overflowing fountain of living water. Let our home be a safe place for anyone and everyone who crosses the threshold. Let me stand as Your son/daughter to be the person where the enemy was defeated and a new history was determined in our family line from this day forward.

Thank You, Lord. Thank You that when we pray, the demonic must obey. Thank You that we have Your power and authority, because Jesus, You died and then rose to victory. We claim that victory over divorce for ourselves, our children and our children's children to a thousand generations in accordance with Your Holy Word.

Today we now celebrate as a mighty move of God has begun, and we can't wait to see the lives and marriages You save just because we asked. You love us that much.

We adore You. Let our worship destroy the enemy. Let our love shine as bright as the noonday sun as we love our family and our neighbors. In the Most Powerful Name Above All Names. JESUS, AMEN!

About Lynn Donovan

Lynn Donovan is the co-author of *Winning Him Without Words & Not Alone*. She has been married to her husband, Mike, for 25 years. She is an ordinary woman with a passion to lead believers to walk in

God's truth and the love and healing of Jesus Christ through the power of the Holy Spirit. She's been a guest on 700 Club Interactive, Focus on the Family, Dr. Dobson's FamilyTalk and FamilyLife Today. Her consuming desire is that every believer THRIVES in the freedom, authority and power of her inheritance in Jesus Christ. Lynn lives with husband in Temecula, California. Visit Lynn at SpirituallyUnequalMarriage.com or Lynn Donovan.org.

Bless and Pray Over Your Marriage Bed
By Dineen Miller

I am my beloved's and my beloved is mine.
— Song of Solomon 6:3 (ESV)

No matter which end of the aisle you're on—bride or groom—the day we say "I do" is the moment a covenant is created both in the natural and the spiritual realms. There is a holiness that comes from this union that is designed to bring two people into the closest relationship we will have on this earth and is symbolic of the bride of Christ and marriage feast to come with Jesus' return.

In other words, it's a big deal! And there is no place more in need of prayer in a marriage than the marriage bed. The physical and spiritual union of a couple is precious and needs protection and blessing.

"But at the beginning of creation God 'made them male and female.' 'For this reason a man will leave his father and mother and be united to his wife, and the two will become one flesh.' So they are no longer two, but one flesh. Therefore what God has joined together, let no one separate." — Mark 10:6-9

The wonderful outcome of this intentional prayer is greater intimacy and connection. I've prayed and blessed my marriage bed, our bedroom, our time together and even our romance. God's love and provision cover all His creation and sexual intimacy between a husband and wife is part of that.

Father God, thank You for the blessing of sexual intimacy that You have created for marriage—for a husband and wife. In the name of Jesus, I bless my marriage bed with tenderness, love, peace and protection. I declare this room and bed off limits to anything that would interfere with God's plan and design for marriage—anything that would attempt to separate what God has made as one. (Bind as needed, in the name of Jesus: impure thoughts, past harms or hurts, pornography, adultery, manipulation, control, bitterness or unforgiveness). I declare in the name of Jesus that we are one and that nothing can separate or come between my spouse and me.

In the name of Jesus, I declare our bedroom and intimate time together to be protected and blessed. Lord, I ask for the Holy Spirit inspiration to love my spouse well and without hesitation or reservation. I ask that anything in my heart that needs healing or to be removed be done by Your loving hand. I pray against and bind anything that interferes, hinders or comes between my spouse and I and our time together. And I commit this time to be an opportunity to love my spouse with my heart, my body, my soul and my spirit.

Lord Jesus, I pray most of all that this act of love would touch my spouse's heart deeply with the depth and reality of God's love for us, for my spouse, and His heart for our marriage. In the name of Jesus, amen!

About Dineen Miller

Dineen Miller is passionate about God's Word and truth. She's been featured on the Moody Radio Network, Focus on the Family Radio, Dr. James Dobson's FamilyTalk, FamilyLife Today and INSIGHT on Miracle Channel. Dineen is the coauthor of the award-winning book, *Winning Him Without Words* and *Not Alone: Trusting God to Raise Godly Kids in a Spiritually Mismatched Home*. She is also the author of the ACFW Carol Award winning book, *The Soul Saver*. She and her husband love to collect shells and walk the famous white sands of Siesta Key Beach, Florida. Visit Dineen online at SpirituallyUnequalMarriage.com and DineenMiller.com.

Faith For Cornelius

By Tara Altay

How a Christian and a Muslim agree to marry one another is a story for another day. The promise and guide to praying for my husband came shortly after we shared our vows. We married in a quaint seashore bed and breakfast with our closest friends and family in attendance.

In the weeks following our wedding, an understanding slowly came into focus in my gut and spirit. I wasn't anxious or afraid anymore about the salvation of my husband and our children. Or was I, perhaps, becoming lax in my zeal for God, or worse, deceived because we were "unequally yoked?" This concern moved me to scour the Word for truth.

I went to the first verse I recalled:

They replied, "Believe in the Lord Jesus, and you will be saved—you and your household." — Acts 16:31

Streams of other verses and stories showered my spirit. God is thorough and snuffs out any remaining embers of doubt with the fresh spring rainfall of His Word. I wasn't deceived or lazy. God had given me the gift of faith for my whole family's salvation!

For the unbelieving husband has been sanctified through his wife, and the unbelieving wife has been sanctified through her believing husband. Otherwise your children would be unclean, but as it is, they are holy. — 1 Corinthians 7:14

He will bring you a message in which you and your whole household will be saved. — Acts 11:14

Often, when I pray these and other verses for my husband, I sense they are more a reminder and encouragement to me than actual requests to God. God's promises trump our fears with certainty and finality.

These verses weren't all God had in mind, however. He intended to be very personal with a prayer for my husband.

Three years after exchanging vows with my awesome husband, I was reading Mark Batterson's, *The Circle Maker*. He encourages his readers to dream big. "I can dream big," I thought with excitement! "But what to dream? There are so many possibilities."

As I asked God about what I should dream. I sensed it was my husband's salvation. Honestly, I was a little disappointed. I thought I already believed this for him and thought God could do something a little bigger. If I'm honest still, I was disappointed because I wanted the "big thing" to be more about me. Yuck, I know. Thankfully God doesn't hold a grudge and we forged ahead into the surprise He had planned.

I read the story of Cornelius—possibly the first non-Jewish convert—in Acts 10-11.

A Summary of Cornelius's Side of the Story...

Devout family guy, not Christian or Jewish. He faithfully prayed and gave generously to the poor. An angel comes to him saying, "God remembers you. Send for Peter in Joppa, and by the way, he is at Simon the Tanner's house."

Cornelius immediately obeys, likely because he was a respected military officer which prompts this 'no excuse' obedience. His noble character and career spoke to me about my husband.

My husband is a Turkish-born American citizen. He was raised and nurtured in a close-knit, devout Muslim home for 19 years until he moved to the United States. He came to this country alone, speaking only Turkish. He worked and studied and eventually became an exceptional physician. He is quiet, humble, kind, patient and faithful. As they say, opposites attract.

On a rooftop, God spoke to Peter in a vivid vision, using his current natural hunger to reveal a spiritual truth. God shows Peter a table full of all food, especially highlighting foods He previously called filthy. "You can eat it now, it's clean, it won't hurt you or mess up your reputation, I promise!" *(Author's translation, Acts 11:9).*

The profound implication of forfeiting prejudices and marginalizing certain people is littered throughout this story. More personally, however, the GOD I know SEES my sweet Muslim husband.

If remembering this non-believer wasn't enough, God sends this real life friend of Jesus and a founder of the first Christian church to Cornelius's house. He shares the Good News with him and leads his whole family to receive the Holy Spirit.

The story is a gushing ocean-wave to my spirit. Sometimes I just shout the name of Cornelius in my spirit. God and I both know what that prayer means.

To solidify this in my heart, God sent another confirmation.

The back story to how I received my copy of *The Circle Maker* began as we were moving to a new state, and I had a new church picked out, so I thought. On the day we moved, my dear friend and faithful prayer partner, Emily, gave me a copy of the book. I thought I had a pretty aggressive prayer life until I read it.

A couple of chapters in, I realized Pastor Mark's church was within minutes of our new home. I hadn't finished the book yet when we started attending National Community Church. The day after receiving this prayer for my husband, I was reading Mark Batterson's book. Not only did the book reference the story of Cornelius, but sometimes Pastor Mark actually prays on a rooftop! Like Peter!

When I read about Pastor Mark's roof top prayer sessions, I immediately and frantically wanted to send an email prayer request and a box of chalk. "Please, draw some circles around my husband up there, Pastor Mark!" I didn't send the crazy request, but I was filled with hope by all the quirky confirmations the Lord sent me.

Cornelius, Lord! Thank You for seeing and promising to save my Cornelius. . .and our whole household!

About Tara Altay

Our spiritually and culturally diverse family is nestled in for the long haul in Northern Virginia. I am thankful to hail from the great state of New Jersey and fortunate to be married to my kind, patient and handsome husband from Turkey. We have three awesome little girls who are as diverse in personality as my husband and I are in culture and spirituality. Life for us is rich and colorful on our good days and character building on our hard days! It's all worth it!

Praying After Divorce
By Lynette Duquette

Father, I thank You that although my marriage has ended, You are now my husband in every way. You are my provider, my protector, the lover of my soul. While I grieve over the end of my marriage, there are times in Your infinite wisdom and sovereignty that You say no to restoration. You see my future and have something better in mind. Forgive me, Lord, if I ever made my marriage an idol, focusing too much on saving it that I lost sight of You and Your plan for me as an individual.

Father, I ask You to open my husband's/wife's eyes, ears and heart to the truth of who You are, and how much You love him/her. If he/she is involved in another relationship, I pray for Your truth to reach that person also. I pray that Your Holy Spirit would pierce their hearts and if they are involved in sexual sin, that You would bring conviction. Jesus died on the cross for them as much as He did for me, and if they repent, I know, Lord, that they too can spend eternity with You. I ask you, Lord, to bless them in every area of their life, Lord, for it is the kindness of God that leads to repentance.

Lord, if I have contact with my spouse and his/her new partner, give me the power to be gracious and kind.

Father, thank You for the time I had with my spouse. I have been blessed with a wonderful child(ren) through this relationship. May my child(ren) continue to have a relationship with him/her all under Your protective hand.

Thank You, Lord, for all You have done through this journey of my marriage and separation. Thank You for the lessons, the trials and even the pain, through which You have molded and shaped me. I will continue to lean on You and seek You with all my heart. In Jesus' name, amen!

About Lynette Duquette

Lynette lives in Massachusetts and after separating from her husband started college —a dream she put on hold for a long time. She has a son who lives in Washington and plans to start her own ministry in the future.

Conclusion

By Lynn Donovan

Jesus said, "I will give you the keys of the kingdom of heaven; whatever you bind on earth will be bound in heaven, and whatever you loose on earth will be loosed in heaven."
— Matthew 16:19

In a rare and vivid dream, Jesus was before me. In His hand were three large iron and ancient keys. He held them out to me and bid me receive them. In that moment, the passage, Matthew 16:19 became powerful and relevant in my life. Yet it was a year later when reading through the book of Romans that the Holy Spirit revealed the significance of each key and what they unlocked.

For the kingdom of God is not a matter of eating and drinking, but of righteousness, peace and joy in the Holy Spirit. —Romans 14:17

It felt as though I was struck by lightning as understanding flooded my mind and spirit. The Kingdom of God is righteousness (goodness), peace and joy. The keys Jesus entrusted to me were keys to release Kingdom attributes into our lives, right now, on earth.

Goodness, peace and joy.

My faith, my entire life, altered through the understanding of these two passages. I now live to release those facets of the Kingdom into my life and those with whom I have contact. I pray that you have received all of these attributes as your read through this collection of teachings and prayers. They are a love offering to our King!

I earnestly pray that you have received supernatural tools that change your prayer life and then use your words to impact your life, marriage, family and the world for Jesus Christ.

The Power of Prayer

Are any of you suffering hardships? You should pray. Are any of you

*happy? You should sing praises. Are any of you sick? You should call for
the elders of the church to come and pray over you, anointing you with oil
in the name of the Lord. Such a prayer offered in faith will heal the sick,
and the Lord will make you well. And if you have committed any sins, you
will be forgiven.*

*Confess your sins to each other and pray for each other so that you
may be healed. The earnest prayer of a righteous person has great power
and produces wonderful results. —James 5:13-16*

The utterances of a heart and life sold out for God are powerful
indeed. Allow the truth of the Word to fill your heart with hope and life
with purpose. Pray with belief, courage and conviction. Engage your will
and passions and speak the Word out through your prayers. Remember
you bear the image of the Living God. What you speak releases life and
power. They are powerful to bring down even mighty strongholds.

*We are human, but we don't wage war as humans do. We use
God's mighty weapons, not worldly weapons, to knock down the
strongholds of human reasoning and to destroy false arguments.
We destroy every proud obstacle that keeps people from knowing
God. We capture their rebellious thoughts and teach them to
obey Christ. — 2 Corinthians 10:3-5*

I pray a blessing of joy, peace, and righteousness over you (Romans 14:17). In Jesus' name. AMEN!

With eternal love, your sister, Lynn Donovan

"Moving. Challenging. Full of devastating, healing truth."

Ten Christ centered keys to thriving in a spiritual mismatch. God wants every marriage to exude peace and love, and *Winning Him Without Words* empowers readers to create that environment in their homes and thrive as God works.

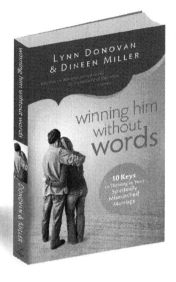

"This book by far has been the most helpful, the most rewarding, the most convicting, and the one that makes the most sense!"
— Debra Alley, Small Group Leader

"This book helped me to understand the impact a believing wife can have on her unbelieving spouse."
— Susan, Reader

"The book was liberating."
— Donna, Reader

"This book spoke straight to my heart and addressed many of the issues I am facing in my marriage. The honesty poured straight from the heart of these two authors."
— Dawn, Reader

"This book came at a time in my life that I really needed it and I couldn't be more thankful to both Lynn and Dineen for baring their souls and helping those of us in unequally yoked marriages. I know now that I am not alone!"
— Sherrie, Reader

"I was very excited as a Pastor's wife and Women's Ministry Leader to get this book. I can't wait to pass it on to ladies in my church and in our community."
— Abbie, Reader and pastor's wife

"Unequally yoked marriages are something all counselors encounter... We are trained to bring up the "hot button" issues like children, finances, and faith during premarital counseling... Both authors are so candid throughout the book that I never felt like this was just another Christian self-help book."
— Jeannie M. Campbell, Licensed Marriage and Family Therapist

"What is amazing about this book is that the Ten Keys will not only improve any marriage, they will bring you closer to God."
— Amazon reader and reviewer

www.SpirituallyUnequalMarriage.com

"The most improtant parenting advice that I have every received."

This is a parenting book, but it's much more. It's a love letter to all mothers—a message that changes our homes, our kids and our lives. It's about the Father's love that impacts those around us and changes ordinary moms into women of extraordinarygrace, beauty and wisdom.

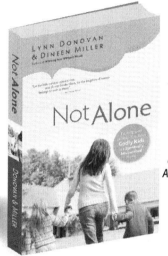

Living in a spiritually mismatched marriage represents one of the greatest challenges a couple can face. Lynn Donovan and Dineen Miller tackle the issue head-on with grace, honesty, and a wealth of practical advice. I'm encouraged by their willingness to reach out to this often-overlooked segment of the Church.
— Jim Daly, President, Focus on the Family

The authors are transparent in this book. There are stories of triumph as well as heartbreak. I laughed. I cried. I related to the experiences these women shared. As I was reading, I learned a lot about parenting – being authentic, intentional, and not having to "do it all."
— Bekcy Jo

This book is filled with real-life stories of brokenness, hope, encouragement, and most of all God's love for us all. The authors have made themselves vulnerable and in return God has blessed them with the words in this book. Living in a spiritually mismatched marriage and raising my young children has often left me feeling desperate and alone. The peace and comfort I gained from this book has given me a sense of overwhelming hope and strength to push forward. I have been reminded to pray more deeply and passionately for my children. As I read the book, I was able to immediately put into action the practical guidance and advice provided by the authors. "Not Alone" is a must read for any parent raising children in today's broken world.
— Amazon Reader

I've read tons of women's bible studies and parenting books but this is the first one that has been specifically written for me as an un-equally yoked wife. Not Alone was written by two women that have walked this path and are willing to share every lesson they've learned along the way. The book addresses our most honest questions and deepest fears in a way that's encouraging and never condemning. Each chapter ends with a section of questions that are perfect for individual quiet time or small group discussions. At its core, the book teaches that the most important thing that we can do for our kids is love Jesus with every bit of our being. One of the big lessons for me was that God wants to partner with me to raise my kids and he loves them more than I can possibly imagine. I would encourage every mother to read this one, because it contains the most important parenting advice that I have ever received.
— Momof2

www.SpirituallyUnequalMarriage.com

Made in the USA
Middletown, DE
27 December 2016